The Giftionary

ST. MARTIN'S GRIFFIN'S  NEW YORK

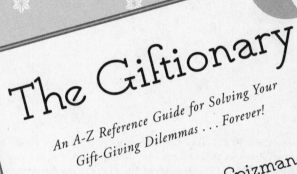

The Giftionary

An A-Z Reference Guide for Solving Your
Gift-Giving Dilemmas . . . Forever!

Robyn Freedman Spizman

www.stmartins.com

Book design by Ellen Cipriano

LIBRARY OF CONGRESS CATALOGING-IN-PUBLICATION DATA

Spizman, Robyn Freedman.
    The giftionary ; an A-Z reference guide for solving your gift-giving dilemmas forever! /
Robyn Freedman Spizman.—1st ed.
      p. cm.
    ISBN 0-312-31190-7
    1. Gifts. I. Title.
GT3040.S68 2003
394—dc21

                                          2002045223

10 9 8 7 6 5 4 3 2

This book is dedicated to the school of thought
That the lessons of giftgiving can surely be taught.
So here's the secret to give you a start . . .
When giving a gift, begin with your heart.

—RFS—

Contents

Acknowledgments

My heartfelt appreciation goes to the most precious gifts in my life—my family and friends. To Willy (a gift of a husband) and our best gifts ever—our children, Justin and Ali—your precious presence makes my life totally worthwhile. To my devoted parents, Phyllis and Jack Freedman, for their endless gifts of wisdom and a lifetime of unconditional love, and thank you to my brother Doug (Ferrari Freedman) and his real-life Genie (a pure saint), and to Sam, Aunt Lois and Uncle Jerry Blonder, Aunt Ramona Freedman, and my entire family. To my beloved grandparents and family no longer present, you will always be in my heart. And to Bettye Storne and Mary Billingsley—our real-life angels. You are all the very best gifts life has to offer!

To my dedicated literary agent and wonderful friend, Meredith Bernstein (the smartest resource I know!), thank you for your unwavering friendship and unending confidence. To St. Martin's Press-ents: Matthew Shear (publisher extraordinaire), Jennifer Enderlin (my gifted editor), John Karle (the ultimate publicist), and Kimberly Cardascia for your wonderful assistance. To Paige Janco, a gift to the Spizman Agency, and to Suzi Brozman, for your wonderful assistance.

A heartfelt thanks goes to my remarkable friend and stylist, Jack Morton (a gift of talent to so many), and his amazing team at Indulgence Salon. To the salt of the earth birthday club and their perfect partners—friends whom I cherish beyond words: Patty and Larry Brown, Ava and Bob Wilensky, Gail and Lyons Heyman, Betty and Alan Sunshine, Lorie and Arthur Simon, Nancy and Wayne Freedman, Norma and Peter Gordon, Shirley and Barry Retter, and Donna and Michael Weinstock. And to my treasured lifelong friends: my childhood confidant Carla (and Ralph) Lovell, Linda (and Howard) Reisman, Lorie Lewis (and Les Fuchs), Marianne and Stephen Garber, Laurie Selzer, Marla Shavin, Viki

Freeman, Janie Fishman, JacLynn Morris, Lisa Karesh, Terry Spector, Wendy Light, Susan Silber, Mr. Pepe, Miss Ray, and all of my Margaret Mitchell Buds—friends forever!

To my *Women for Hire* coauthor and career fair guru, my friend for life and shopping diva, Tory Johnson—and to CMI legend and author Bruce T. Blythe—you are both rare gifts life offers while at work. My endless thanks to PTA's Rick Frishman, the unstoppable Hillary Rivman, and Kristin Clifford for your support and confidence—you guys are the best. To my friends at WXIA TV: my incredible cohost, Tiffany Cochran, and my gifted producers, Aviva Hoffman, Kalina Haynes, Kerry Oslund, and Ann Shelton. And to Mary Lynn Ryan, Judy Fortin, Joanne LaMarca, and Betsy Alexander—you are gifts to anyone who has the pleasure of working with you. An awe-inspiring thanks to my friends and talented authors who inspire us all: H. Jackson and Rosemary Brown, Jr., Stedman Graham, and Mark Victor Hansen.

To Doug Isenberg, Steven M. Winter, Adrian Grant, Brad Berman, and Bruce Weinstein for their expert advice, and to my extended family and endless circle of friends, including Nancy Joffre, Harriett Bavarsky, Arlene Hoffman, Lala Gossen, Molly Stryer, Janie Fishman, the Fritz family, Tracy Green, Kieth Saxe, Narvie Harris, Leslie Isenberg, Dale Dyer, the Cohens, my Atlanta and Tennessee cousins, Dr. David Garber, Dr. Ronald Goldstein, Desiree Landers, Sheila Shechtman, Laura Weiss, Dawn Foster, Tim Hayes, Art Evans, Amanda Perkins, Tracy Green, and Barbara Cochran Berry.

And last but not least, to the many readers who have read and shared my books for decades, you honor me with your continued presence.

Introduction

Welcome to *The Giftionary*, your year-round source for giftgiving. Like a dictionary, you'll find gifts arranged by topics in an A-to-Z fashion for every occasion. Jam packed with extraordinary and clever ideas, this book will provide years of gift ideas, memorable moments, words that are free and fabulous, and helpful tips to make you look like a gift-giving and memory-making pro!

As a consumer advocate for over two decades, a nationally known gift-giving expert, and the author of more than seventy books, I have discovered endless ideas that take giftgiving to greater heights. It's a talent to match up the recipient with the perfect gift, but the real secret to being a gifted giver is to avoid trying to read someone's mind. It's about understanding what he or she values. If you really are dedicated to giving a present someone will enjoy and adore, then find out their likes and dislikes ahead of time. The goal is to discover what makes them feel special, loved, and adored. Sometimes it's words of thanks, praise, or a gift from the heart, while at other times it's a gift that is totally indulgent.

To accomplish this goal, begin inquiring when they least expect it. Quiz them about their favorite color, worst gift they've ever been given, objects they collect, and special interests. Do they value gifts, or are they a sentimentalist and prefer heartfelt words, charitable donations, or good deeds? And when giving a gift, always reflect the recipient's taste, not just yours.

With the help of *The Giftionary*, you will escape the gift-giving blues. There's also a special section for recording your VIP information, favorite resources, and those can't-miss moments. The quick-glance, easy-to-use index is arranged by theme, interest, and occasion to instantly help you find gift ideas even for the hard-to-please as well as what to say when you're at a loss for words. Take it from me. Being prepared for those gift-giving emergencies with a gift closet stocked up with your favorite last-minute gifts is essential. On-the-go giftgivers are always pre-pared and now, with the help of this book, you will be, too.

The Giftionary is standing by ready to help you out in a gift-giving emergency. I sincerely hope it will help you mark the occasion with meaningful gestures and make your giftgiving, party-planning, thank-you-note writing, and expressions of gratitude and affection effortless.

Happy giftgiving!

A

Is for Anniversary

Anniversaries are our way of marking life's special occasions. From first dates to fiftieth wedding anniversaries, imaginative and appropriate gifts make every milestone more memorable. Anniversaries are a ready-made excuse for a party, a gift, an indulgence of passion and pizzazz. Let your imagination run wild as you honor a special day and the celebrants!

Whether you are celebrating your own anniversary and trying to figure out what to give your partner, or you want to select the perfect gift for a special couple, anniversary gifts should be both useful and make each moment momentous. Anniversary gifts, like wedding gifts, should also reflect the taste of the recipients. What might be perfect for one couple could be considered a white elephant to another, so think before you purchase.

First Wedding Anniversary

Wear Your Heart on Your Sleeve. Let your anniversary gift to your mate express your love and make the day a flurry of hearts. A box of candy, a heart-shaped cake, heart-shaped doilies, and a heart-shaped necklace wrapped in a heart-shaped box on her nightstand. If you're a passable cook, make a heart-shaped meatloaf, or surprise him with breakfast in bed with heart-shaped pancakes with raspberry syrup. Follow the theme with a menu of hearts—from a hearts of palm salad to an artichoke-heart pizza. Don't forget a little silver, gold, or diamond heart pinned to your sleeve, especially for her.

For Your Leading Lady. Show how much you love her or him by purchasing tickets to a special play and then enclosing them in a card that says, "To my leading lady."

Anniversary Gifts by Years

YEAR	TRADITIONAL	MODERN
1st year	Paper, plastic	Clock
2nd	Cotton	China
3rd	Leather	Crystal, glass
4th	Linen, silk, flowers, fruit	Appliances
5th	Wood	Silverware
6th	Candy, iron	Wood
7th	Copper, wool	Desk sets
8th	Bronze, pottery	Linens, lace
9th	Pottery, willow	Leather, china, glass
10th	Tin, aluminum	Diamond jewelry
11th	Steel	Fashion jewelry
12th	Linen, silk	Pearls, nylon
13th	Lace	Furs, textiles
14th	Ivory	Gold jewelry
15th	Crystal, glass	Watch
20th	China	Platinum
25th	Silver	Silver
30th	Pearl	Diamond jewelry
35th	Jade, coral	Jade
40th	Ruby, garnet	Ruby
45th	Sapphire	Sapphire
50th	Gold	Gold
55th	Emerald, turquoise	Emerald
60th	Diamond	Diamond or gold
75th	Diamond	Diamond

First Things First. Paper is the traditional first-anniversary gift. But not just any paper. Be creative. Think of a paper-themed deluge of gifts. Include a newspaper from the wedding day, his and her magazine subscriptions, a photo album with highlights of the anniversary couple's first year of wedded bliss, a colored and embellished wedding invitation framed with their wedding portrait. Make it a picture-perfect day with a gift certificate for a portrait, either painted or photographed.

Back to the Future. Choose a stock, one that's solid and dependable. Buy a single share. Then each year, celebrate your anniversary with another share. If you're a romantic fool, earmark the proceeds of this fund for a glamorous anniversary, say a Silver- or Golden-Anniversary cruise. If you're the practical type, save it for a retirement fund, a twilight-years cottage, or college for the kids.

Lasting Treasures. Engrave a gift with a romantic message. Add a special ILY (I love you) to the inside of his wedding band without him knowing it, or select a piece of jewelry for her where you can add a special phrase like "Forever yours" (with your name or initials side-by-side).

Recreate Her Bouquet. When you send flowers, select the flowers that she included in her bridal bouquet. Remember your first anniversary by sending her a dozen flowers with each flower representing a month you've shared as husband and wife. And don't forget to tell her you would marry her all over again. This is a lovely tradition to repeat each year and call it "your anniversary bouquet."

The Time of Their Lives. Modern gifting declares clocks the choice of the day for a first anniversary. Let yours say, "Time Flies When You're Having Fun" with a beautiful watch to commemorate your love. His and hers matching wristwatches are a great gift to select together. Or, if your mate's a good sport, tell him so with a casual sports watch.

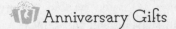 Anniversary Gifts

A Together Gift. When you don't know what to give each other, select a gift you want together. Call it your "together gift" and choose a gift you'll both enjoy, from a new television set, to a piece of art for your home, to a fabulous trip to a faraway place. It's also a great way to build a collection of something that gives you pleasure year round.

Calling All Friends. Orchestrate a battery of phone calls from friends and family, old and new. This one could take some planning: Assign times throughout the day and evening to delight the happy couple with their friends' attention.

The Perfect Pair. Tell the couple they are the perfect pair and suited for each other with a gift of two of anything from a pair of candlesticks, a pair of his and her bathrobes, or even a bicycle built for two. Add a note that says, "It takes two things to make a great marriage— the two of you!"

Eatings Greetings. Purchase gift certificates to a variety of restaurants in their neighborhood, or if possible, choose one for each letter of the word *love*. (*L* is for Luigies, *O* is for the Old Green Inn . . .) This will take some creative thinking, but you'll be surprised how many choices are available.

The Anniversary Book. Fill a scrapbook, year by year, with favorite pictures of the married couple. This idea works best if you start it when a couple is first married and add to it yearly. Before you know it, they'll be married for quite a few years and your gift will be a treasured keepsake.

Silver Anniversary Plus

Catch a Falling Star and Put It in Your Pocket. Or better yet, leave the stars in the heavens, but designate one as your very own and give her a star-shaped necklace. It's the sentiment that counts here. Then share how you'd move heaven and earth for your heaven-sent, angel of a wife.

Now and Then. They haven't gotten older, they've gotten better. Tell them so with a selection of gifts from then and now. Wines from their wedding year and an enlarged photograph, taken at the wedding and then one this year, with the inscription, "You haven't gotten older, you've gotten better." Include a book, put together by family and friends, of memories from each of the couple's twenty-five years. And top it all off with the gift of silver, of course. Consider silver dollars, silver serving pieces, silver picture frames, silver cuff links, or a sterling-engraved locket on a chain with a picture of the two of them tucked inside.

Happily Ever After. Interview the couple about all the most meaningful times in their lives and what they want their grandchildren to know about them. Give this gift with copies made for their children and then, one day, their grandchildren.

Simply Silver. For a married couple, reaching their twenty-fifth anniversary is an awesome accomplishment. They've survived it all . . . together. Celebrate that togetherness with gifts that say, "You've made it!" The night before deliver a basket of bagels, pastries, juice, and coffee for a relaxing breakfast in bed. Treat them to a day at the spa together, complete with dinner, or a picnic dinner and tickets to their favorite outdoor venue, a bottle of vintage champagne, a pair of crystal flutes, and an indulgent box of chocolates.

A Silver Sunset Spectacular. Plan a gala silver anniversary party for loved ones. Make silver the theme of the evening. Give guests silver party hats, and toast the couple with silver champagne flutes. Ask guests to bring theme gifts rather than expensive ones: twenty-five reasons they're friends, twenty-five memories, twenty-five photos, twenty-five lines of a favorite romantic poem, all of which you can videotape for a priceless gift for the honorees. And don't forget the music . . . "Sail Along Silver Moon" and "By the Light of the Silvery Moon."

Music to Our Ears. For our twenty-seventh wedding anniversary, our children put together a CD filled with romantic songs. It was a gift that we treasured because they chose lyrics that reflected our love for each other.

The "I Love You" Jar. Tell your spouse how special he or she is, even after twenty-five, thirty or any number of years together. Use a clean, empty coffee jar or purchase a pretty clear glass vase. On slips of paper like in fortune cookies, write dozens of reasons you adore your mate. Fold them and fill up the jar with your display of affection. Add a bow and a note telling your spouse to select one a day. This is also a wonderful gift from a group of friends, a loving sibling, or grandchildren.

Do As the Romans Do. In Roman numerals, *L* is the symbol for fifty. Fill the anniversary couple's day with *L*'s. Bring them gifts of love and laughter. Give her lace, a lapis bracelet, a lavender sachet, a luxurious lunch, and lessons in something she's interested in. Give him something made from leather, a day at the lake or on the golf links. If you're so moved, write a letter and let them know that *L* stands for their long-standing love and how they've inspired you.

Stamp of Approval. Visit a stamp store and find a beautiful stamp issued in the wedding year. Have it mounted and framed, and present it with a card that says, "You two have my lifetime stamp of approval." Or select fifty love-themed stamps and add the message, "Happy Fiftieth Anniversary . . . let's stick together for fifty more!"

Come As You Were. Throw an anniversary party everyone will rave about. Make it memorable, make it theirs alone, a "come as you were" party. Invite friends to wear vintage clothing from the wedding era, blow up photos of the newlyweds into posters for everyone to sign. Serve wedding cake and champagne. Assemble as many of the wedding party as possible and pose for a photo update. Present the "bride" with a copy of her bouquet. Use wedding favors and decorations to highlight the joy of the occasion. While they are in the party, have a sign added to their car that says, "Just (Happily) Married!"

Aloha. What more fitting destination for the fiftieth anniversary couple than a getaway to the fiftieth state? Hawaii's aloha spirit beckons. Announce the trip with an orchid for her, a golf club for him, a tube of suntan oil, and a promise of romance and heavenly adventure. Head for the bright lights of Oahu, Waikiki Beach, and the Arizona Memorial at Pearl Harbor. Then whisk them away for quiet days on the sun-drenched beaches of Maui or Kauai.

B

Is for Birthdays Gifts

Most of us think of our birthdays as the most special, personal day of the whole year. Being the center of attention has its advantages, but how do you make that special day worth waiting for? All you need is a little thought and a little creativity. From sweet sixteen, to turning twenty-one, and onward to those really big ones, birthday gifts can be so special and don't need to cost a fortune.

The key to giving great birthday gifts is to really observe a person's likes and dislikes. Even when they say, "Don't make a fuss," be sure to read between the lines. You can never make someone feel too special, so go for it and make his or her birthday extraspecial and the best ever!

Children's Birthdays

Rub-A-Dub-Tub. Give a basket of tub-friendly toys, including bath crayons, nonirritating bubble bath, a boat, rubber ducky (every kid should have one), and a basketball hoop with suction cups to stick on the side of the tub. Roll it all up in a bathtowel embroidered with the birthday child's name and add ribbons.

Aisles of Smiles. On the day of his birthday take a child to a toy store and let him select a toy or two after carefully reviewing all the aisles. Once he narrows his choices and makes his selection, plan to spend an afternoon or evening with him to make sure everything works and he knows how to operate each toy. Your undivided attention and time will be the best gift of all.

Stocking Up. Here's a gift that keeps on giving. A single share of stock continues to grow through the years, until the child is old enough to really appreciate its value and your thoughtfulness in starting him or her on the road to

Zodiac Signs

January 20 to February 18: Aquarius (the Water Bearer)
February 19 to March 20: Pisces (the Fish)
March 21 to April 19: Aries (the Ram)
April 20 to May 20: Taurus (the Bull)
May 21 to June 21: Gemini (the Twins)
June 22 to July 22: Cancer (the Crab)
July 23 to August 22: Leo (the Lion)
August 23 to September 22: Virgo (the Virgin)
September 23 to October 23: Libra (the Balance)
October 24 to November 21: Scorpio (the Scorpion)
November 22 to December 21: Sagittarius (the Archer)
December 22 to January 19: Capricorn (the Goat)

prosperity. Match the stock to the interests of the child regardless of age. Perhaps the first year is with a favorite company that caters to babies (baby food perhaps?), or a stock to lay the foundation (a home-building-supply company?), an electric company for a busy toddler on the go, or a computer-related stock for a cyber kid. When splurging, match the number of shares to the age of the child.

A Touch of Class. Give a set of classes that inspire a new hobby or talent. From art lessons to music or karate, the key is to match interests that will contribute to a child's self-esteem, personal growth, and development.

You Take the Cake! With a teacher's permission, have the birthday kid's photo transferred to a sheet cake and provide the whole class with a picture-perfect treat to remember. Or, bring loads of gummy worms, crushed chocolate cookies, and toppings for decorating cupcakes right on the spot.

Party Animal. Check with the zoo, and adopt an animal in your child's name. You can make regular visits to check up on your "pet," and you can announce the adoption with a stuffed animal of the same species.

Say "Cheese." Encourage the young photographer with a stack of one-time use cameras and coupons for developing photos or transferring them to CDs. Include a scrapbook and some preaddressed envelopes to send you his or her best photo, if you live far away.

Collection Perfection. Most kids collect something, whether it's baseball cards, cars, dolls, snow globes, or autographs. Inquire what a child collects and add to his collection with a special addition, love from you. Or, if he hasn't started a collection, check out themes of interest and let your gift be the first of many to help build one.

Let the Games Begin. A real big-league jersey, a team hat, seats in the stadium or arena, a program, a ball, and an extra ticket to bring his best friend. Can life get any better?

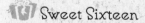 Sweet Sixteen

Queen of Hearts. "Sweet Sixteen" is a once-in-a-lifetime event. Shower her with heart-felt gifts, a cor-

sage of sweetheart roses, a box of heart-shaped candy, and a necklace with a heart-shaped pendant beautifully wrapped and sitting on her night table to surprise her when she wakes up. Don't forget the heart-shaped pancakes and paper crown waiting on the kitchen table.

Sugar and Spice and Everything Nice. Give her a special day at the spa with a makeover, manicure, and pedicure. When it's time for the manicure, bring her best friends for one, too, and end with a private party!

Charmed, I'm Sure. Start a tradition. Give your Sweet Sixteen a charm bracelet with a Sweet Sixteen charm. As the years pass, you can add charms to remind her of special occasions. This will be a gift she can cherish through her whole life.

Spin City. Give your sixteen-year-old his choice of music, and lots of it. If you don't trust your ability to pick out what he'd like, give him gift certificates and a portable CD player.

Pretty in Pink. Let her know just how beautiful she is on this special day with a bouquet of pink rose buds and a note saying, "We're tinkled pink it's your birthday!"

The Key to His Heart. He'd love a Ferrari, but he'll have to settle for the next best thing. Car loving sixteen-year-olds will appreciate a subscription to a car magazine, a personalized key chain, or a replica or photograph of his dream car.

Twenty-first Birthday

A Twenty-one Gum Salute. When our son turned twenty-one, I gave him twenty-one little gifts that had special meaning. It took a few weeks to create this gift, but he loved opening each little package that was numbered one through twenty-one. The first gift was a copy of one of my favorite photographs of him and a note that said, "Have a picture-perfect birthday. My how you've grown!" The second was two things I'd like to forget he did (fell and hit the coffee table, wrecked the car). Three was a thirty-minute prepaid telephone card to call home, since he was at college. Four was a photo of our family of four. Five was a $5 gift certificate to a bookstore for my "novel son." And, of course, twenty-one was twenty-one pack-

ages of his favorite gum for a twenty-one gum salute!

Dough Re Mi. If your young adult is just starting out, give him or her money in increments of twenty-one. Twenty-one pennies, nickels, dimes, quarters, silver dollars, singles, twos, fives, tens . . . or as high as you want to go.

In-Tuition. Many young adults coming out of college at twenty-one are burdened with huge college loans. Start a tuition fund to help defray those costs.

"Balms" Away. It's never too soon to start taking care of your skin. Give a basket of skin-care products, including lip balm, skin cream, SPF 30 suntan lotion, cleansing lotion, shaving cream, and moisturizer. For a special touch, add a gift certificate for a facial.

Hey, Big Spender. Fill a wallet with a gift certificate or gift card tucked inside and some spending cash. Don't forget to add a picture of the entire family. Have the wallet embossed with his initials for a personal touch.

Fortieth Birthdays

We Love You "A-Latte." If he's a coffee fiend, give him a gift that keeps on giving: forty gift certificates for a beverage at his favorite coffee house. Include a book to keep him company while he relaxes with his mocha java half-caf latte.

Stroll Down Memory Lane. Haunt garage sales and thrift shops for books from her childhood. Search out Nancy Drew and Cherry Ames mysteries, the Dick and Jane reading series. Wrap them in paper-bag book covers like she used as a child, and add a big red ribbon. If you want to go that extra mile, have personalized bookplates made that say, "From the library of [name] on the novel occasion of her fortieth year."

Go to Any Lengths to Say Happy Birthday. Purchase a few items that help you measure, from retractable tape measures to rulers, and include a note that reads, "I'd go to any lengths to wish you a happy birthday!"

Calling All Friends. Send a prepaid telephone card to his or her best friends and family who live in other cities so they can call him on his big birthday. From high-school friends to classmates from childhood and college buds to family members, these pre-arranged calls will make him feel really special. Add a sticker to the card that says when and what number to call.

For the Sweetest Friend I Know. Type in the key words *vintage candy* on any search engine on the Internet and check out any of the companies that specialize in candy gifts from the past. Some of them offer an assortment from the '50s, the '60s, and the '70s, crammed with the beloved sweets from childhood. From candy dots to black cows and lemon drops, you can't go wrong with a gift for the sweetest forty-year-old on earth!

Fiftieth Birthdays

How Do I Love Thee? Let Me Count Fifty Ways. Create a book or purchase a ready-made journal or scrapbook filled with beautiful paper and include fifty heartfelt reasons, one per page. For a group gift that will be forever treasured, collectively organize a book, *Why We Love Carla*, and have each person contribute a page commemorating her personal feelings.

Include photographs interspersed throughout commemorating all the loving memories and thoughts that make him or her your most special person in the world.

Focus on Fifty. Here's a creative spin you can use when giving a gift for any big birthday, especially a fiftieth celebration. Begin by selecting and giving a gift that represents each letter of the word *fifty*. For the letter *F*, you could choose flowers. *I* might be ice (diamonds, perhaps?). The second *F* could be fashion, food, or a fun outing. *T* might be a terry-cloth robe or the gift of your time helping her get organized or learn to cook a new recipe. And last but not least, *Y* would be a year's subscription to a favorite magazine or simply your friendship forever.

Fifty Reasons to Love Being Fifty. Here's another jar full of motivational inspiration. Give her a reason a day to celebrate her age. Include reasons like: *I'll never have to be a teenager again; I'm not forgetful, I'm just having a Senior Moment; I'm younger than I look; Those aren't wrinkles, they're character lines; I'm helping conserve energy, I'm having a hot flash!* Make them personal, make them funny, make them fun for her!

A Gift That Keeps on Giving. If she wants to save the world, or make a difference, what better way to honor her intentions than with a $50 donation to her pet cause? A gift in her name will touch her and do good at the same time.

Make It Official. Turning fifty is a right of passage and so is this well-respected membership. A few months before his birthday, be the first to sign him up for membership in AARP. Present it with a bound book filled with things you have researched on the Internet including all the terrific discounts he'll get on hotels, travel, insurance, and more now that he's officially OLD.

Vintage Gear. Know someone with a passion for fashion? While you're at the thrift shops, check out the clothes from way back then. Yesterday's costume jewelry is new again, especially if you can find sweater-pin sets and rhinestone sunglasses! If you find a poodle skirt, you'll know you've hit pay dirt! From platform shoes to go-go boots and ladybug pins, there's something for every fifty-year-old that will take each one of them back to their youth.

Life's a Game. Remember Red Rover, Hopscotch, Old Maid, Jump Rope, Jacks, etc.? Give her a goody bag full of childhood fun and laughter. Include the book *If Life Is a Game, Then These Are the Rules* by Cherie Carter-Scott, Ph.D. for wonderful insights for any age.

The $64,000 Question. Make up a quiz about happenings through her life. You could include world-changing events, teen idols, music, movies, even old boyfriends to show her how varied and rich her life has been. Give her the ultimate quiz at a birthday lunch in her honor and the $64,000 prize that you selected. Excellent choices are nostalgic items like a memorabilia item including a favorite-celebrity-autographed photo, a collection of CDs from the year she was Sweet Sixteen, or even an enlarged photograph of a special memory that you secretly get from a family member and then have framed.

Literatati. Kurt Vonnegut wrote his classic *Breakfast of Champions* to celebrate his own fiftieth birthday. Let his magical words help her celebrate her own magical day.

If Vonnegut's not to her taste, find an assortment of books she would love to read but hasn't had time. Jane Austen, Anne Tyler, Susan Isaacs, and Danielle Steele offer absorbing fiction.

You're Not Getting Better, You're Getting Older. Does she have a fabulous sense of humor? Tickle her funny bone with a medicine basket full of remedies for the aging. The latest wrinkle creams and antigas medications will do the trick.

Read All About It. There are several popular books on the market, all devoted to the woman approaching fifty. Choose Judith Viorst's humorous, lovely volume of poetry, *Forever Fifty*, or her serious volume, *Necessary Losses: The Loves, Illusions, Dependencies, and Impossible Expectations That All of Us Have to Give Up in Order to Grow*. You might opt for Wendy Reid Crisp's *100 Things I'm Not Going to Do Now That I'm over 50*, or *Rules for Aging* by Roger Rosenblatt. Bonnie Miller Rubin's *Fifty on Fifty* and Meredith Books' volume, *Fifty Celebrate Fifty*, give a wide variety of perspectives on aging from women of beauty, spirit, and accomplishment. And for the traveler on your list, check out Joan Rattner Heilman's *Unbelievably Good Deals and Great Adventures That You Absolutely Can't Get Unless You're Over 50.*

A Bright Idea. Shower her with candlelight. Find bunches of quirky and unique candleholders . . . from votives to flower pots, tablespoons, tiny glass boxes, anything to hold a candle. Assemble fifty of them in a basket with fifty candles to brighten her life.

Over the Hill . . . Not! Too many people think fifty is old. Let her know she isn't with an over-the-hill hiking trek with a group of her best friends. It's great exercise and, at the far side of your hill, have a party waiting, complete with champagne for toasting and a limo for the ride back home.

Stamp of Approval. Select fifty love stamps and add the message, *"Happy Fiftieth Birthday. . . . Let's stick together for Fifty more!"*

Celebrate and Duplicate. Pick her favorite nonperishable treat . . . a flavor of bubble gum, truffles, petit fours, assorted chocolates, and put fifty of them in a gorgeous box. Overdoing anything in quantities of fifty (or older) will get

your message across and be a gift he or she will really enjoy.

Party On. Throw her a costume bash, "Come as You Wish You Were," or "Come as You Were Then." Give prizes of old 45-rpm records for the best costumes. Try Post Office, or Spin the Bottle if you dare. Play music from the old days . . . The Stroll, Hand Jive, The Twist, The Mashed Potato, The Locomotion . . . and try to remember how you danced them, and why!

Sweet Sixteen Forever. Make it a magical evening, just like when she turned Sweet Sixteen. A corsage of sweetheart roses, romantic '50s and '60s music, candy and snacks from her teen years, and, if you can find one, a ride in a vintage car from back then. If you've got photos of her, enlarge one as a poster for friends to sign as a birthday card. Serve a cake covered in white frosting with big, gooey, pink-frosting roses and, of course, sixteen candles, while playing, what else? *Sixteen Candles*! Top off the evening with a showing of the movie *Pretty in Pink*.

Remember When. If you're a longtime friend, make up a tribute book filled with reminiscences of friends and family for this important day. Include cherished memories like wedding descriptions, birth announcements, report cards, newspaper clippings, a photo montage. Solicit letters and wishes from those "oldie but goldie" friends living near or faraway. Bind them all in a lovely scrapbook. This is a gift she'll treasure forever.

I Feel Pretty. A basket of beauty supplies will help chase away the birthday blues. Include her favorite makeup and scents, an embroidered handkerchief, perhaps a pair of silk stockings, the latest beauty magazine, and a gift certificate to her hairdresser for a new "do" and makeup application. Include a one-time use camera for before and after shots.

His Outrageous Day Out. Make a list of the things he's always wanted to do, but never dared. Give him the list with your invitation to spend a day doing any one of them. Maybe he'd like to drive a racecar, parasail, bungee jump, throw a pot on a wheel, or ride a roller coaster. Include a copy of Frank Sinatra's "I Did It My Way" and tell him he's "King for a Day."

Clever Is As Clever Does. Give her fifty pieces of string to tie on her finger so she won't forget she's turning fifty; fifty pages of a romance novel to remind her what it was like once upon a time; fifty carrots for her failing eyesight; fifty packets of denture cleaner; fifty bandages; fifty minutes of "Golden Oldies" on a CD.

Mirror Mirror. From antique mirrors that are engraved with her initials to pretty jeweled purse compacts and magnifying glasses as well, there's a mirror for everyone's taste and specific needs. Add a note that says, "Mirror, mirror what do you know? Carla's turning fifty and guess what—it doesn't show."

A Coupon Book for the Anti–Fifty-Year-Old. Have a friend or know someone who is dreading turning fifty? Give her a copy of *Peter Pan* with permission to never grow up. Ultimately, the most important gift you can possibly give is the gift of caring. Tell her, and more importantly, *show* her with a letter or coupon book that you're there for the next fifty years plus! Include rides, a guide for balancing a checkbook, words of encouragement, a shoulder, and more.

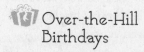

Over-the-Hill Birthdays

Recipes for Love. Find a recipe box, or create one with a 3- by

5-inch-card file. You can paint it with hearts and flowers, or decoupage it, or glue on fabric and jewels. Make it bright and colorful. Fill it with recipes for love from all her friends and family. Give them each a card and ask them to return it to you in time to present it for her birthday. One example: 1 heart full of love, 1 good friend, 1 lifetime of memories. Stir gently and savor. Keeps forever.

Tea for Two. Invite the birthday girl and a group of friends to "High Tea" at the most elegant spot in town. Find one that does it right with tiny sandwiches, cakes, scones, and delicious brewed teas. As a memento of the occasion, each friend could give a lovely cup and saucer as a gift. Don't forget a corsage for the honoree. If she has daughters or granddaughters, this would be a lovely occasion to include them, too.

Mint Condition. Give a proof set of uncirculated coins from her birth year, along with a note that says, "Like these coins, you're still in mint condition, bright as the day you were born."

In Good Company. Find a list of famous people who share his or her birthday. Make a collage with their pictures or with quotes to surround her picture in the center. You could head it, "In Good Company," with the birth date underneath.

Learning Is Forever. Give a catalog of classes being offered in the area. Include art centers, community colleges, business schools, and anything else you think she'd enjoy. Include a card reminding her, "You're not getting older, you're getting smarter," and tell her the first class she signs up for is on you.

Lights, Camera, Action. If you're creative and have a video recorder, make her a movie she'll never get tired of watching. Revisit scenes of her childhood, homes, schools, work places, and get friends to reminisce on camera about her life and theirs. Include her family, teachers, and mentors, too. This kind of living history will be valuable to future generations as well.

Marathon Days. If she doesn't get out much, bring the celebration to her. Include a picnic basket with a special meal of all her favorite treats and add several videos of movies from special times in her life . . . one from each decade, with an emphasis on topics she loves. It could be a theme party with *Love Affair, An Affair to Remember*, and *Sleepless in Seattle*. Or the *Star Wars* trilogy, or a bunch of slapstick comedies. Don't forget the popcorn and candy!

It's Your Day. Make it official. Many mayors, governors, and other politicians are happy to provide a proclamation marking special birthdays and anniversaries. But start early on this one, it could take months to get through the bureaucracy!

C

Is for Career and Hobby Gifts

How can you tell what a person really loves to do? Look at their life choices—what do they do for a living? How do they choose to spend their free time? What are they passionate about? Using careers and hobbies, you'll find a wealth of gift ideas. By matching up their life interests, you can't go wrong. Plus, with a little investigative effort, your thoughtfulness will be greatly appreciated.

The key to giving a career- or hobby-related gift is to consider the person's keen interests. Are they a computer geek or totally low tech? Does he favor a round of golf, or is he a couch potato? Does she love art, to read, or is she an avid antique collector? Whatever the answer, with a little legwork, you are bound to discover related items and interests that will clue you into perfect giftgiving.

Gifts for Grads. If he or she is a recent college graduate, how about giving him a wake-up call? Select a very loud alarm clock and attach a note, "Time for success!" Or, for the college-bound student, consider a gift certificate to an organizing store for those cramped quarters and dorm-room challenges. Or, purchase a prepaid phone card, gift certificate to an online bookstore, or gift card to a DVD rental store located near the college campus.

A Highlighted Gift. Give a copy of *Highlighted in Yellow: A Short Course in Living Wisely and Choosing Well*, by H. Jackson Brown, Jr. and Rochelle Pennington, (Rutledge Hill Press, 2001). Add a package of yellow highlighters and a note that says, "Your accomplishments are highlighted in our hearts. Congratulations."

The Job of Her Dreams. If she's searching for a job, help the job seeker make a great first impression with your gift of personalized stationery on quality paper, just right for résumés and job inquiries. Include a pen and add your own letter, "I've always known you have the 'write' stuff. Hope this helps you land the job of your dreams!" Include a copy of *Women for Hire: The Ultimate Guide to Getting a Job* by Tory Johnson, Robyn Spizman, and Lindsey Pollak, (Perigee, Penguin Putnam, 2002).

It's in the Cards. It's official. He has the job and his very own business cards. Give him a monogrammed card case and tell him, "I knew success was in the cards for you." Or, give a desktop cardholder for her business cards. Have it personalized with her complete name.

A Good Sport. It's easy to find out what your favorite athlete favors. He or she always needs new gear and will appreciate some new clothing. Choose from sweatbands, athletic socks, and T-shirts. Throw in a monogrammed towel and a subscription to a favorite sporting magazine. Or, if you're in doubt, give a gift certificate to a sporting-goods store. Add a note that says, "No sweat . . . just enjoy your special day" or, "Hope your birthday's no sweat!"

Desk Dazzlers. If you're looking for a gift for someone who is devoted to their deskjob, from your accountant, or insurance broker, or the work-at-home type, choose an assortment of matching-metal office essentials . . . a desk calendar, pen-and-pencil set, stapler, notepad, scissors, and metal ruler, all tucked into a wire-mesh office trash can. Add a note that says, "When you put the petal to the medal, I hope you'll enjoy these gifts." There are also endless styles of paperweights, handsome desk sets, and gadgets that will dazzle and jazz up any desk.

Compute This Gift. Investigate the latest gadgets for computer lovers, but don't overlook simple things like a wrist-rest and wireless mouse. Or, check out a specially designed computer chair that's good for your back. One of my favorite suggestions is to give a house call from a reputable computer expert, just in case of an emergency computer glitch.

A Writer's Paradise. Know a wordsmith? Whether it's someone who writes for a living or just enjoys putting words on paper, consider a bag filled with tools for the writer, ranging from a rhyming dictionary to a slang dictionary, thesaurus, and a beautiful notebook embossed with his initials.

Heigh-Ho, Heigh-Ho, It's Off to Work We Go. Find out how she gets to work, and offer a month's worth of commuting. It could be bus or train passes, highway-toll tokens, or a parking pass. Tell her, "Way to go!"

Apple for the Teacher. Involve the entire class and ask each student to contribute a gift based on the theme of apples. Suggest they search for anything unique that has to do with apples, except the real thing. Fill a gift basket chock full of unique apple surprises . . . stationery with apples on it, apple butter, cinnamon apple tea, a box of apple-flavored candies and apple-cider mix. Last but not least, throw in some crunchy fresh apples and add a note that says, "You are the apple of our eye."

Picture This. Teachers love to keep a photographic record of their years in the classroom. Get a group of parents together and give that fabulous teacher a disposable camera and coupons for developing her pictures, or a digital camera.

In a League of His Own. Give your coach a pair of tickets to a professional game or a gift certificate to his favorite sporting-goods store. Tape them to a ball signed by the whole team with a note saying, "Coach, you're in a league of your own!"

What's Up, Doc? Doctors, dentists and healthcare professionals have outside interests and hobbies, so check out what's hanging around the office or ask the staff. From golf mementoes to travel photographs, be observant. Consider a related magazine subscription that, when he finishes reading, his patients could also enjoy in the waiting room. Or, if he or she is a connoisseur of fine wines, orchids, or has a favorite brand of caviar, make a note of it and each year give the preferred selection. If you're still at a loss for what to select, find out if he's involved in a charitable organization and make a donation in his honor.

Just What the Doctor Ordered. When you visit the doctor's office, she's the one you think of, but don't forget the staff. A kind "thank you" to them is especially welcome. Bring a jar of hard candy with a note that says, "To the sweetest staff on earth. This gift will be refilled when The Spizmans return!"

Attorney-Client Privilege. Tell your lawyer it's a privilege doing business with him with a gift of a chocolate torte. He'll appreciate the pun, and the delicious taste of a layered cake, beautifully wrapped and presented with a silver cake server. Or, arrange with his secretary to borrow a snapshot of his family and have it enlarged and printed in black and white and then frame it for his desk. For a humorous gift certain to put a smile on his face, give a super-hero toy with a note that says, "To my favorite super-hero. Thank you for coming to my rescue!"

Community Protectors. From fire fighters to policemen and policewomen, there are many gifts that are appropriate when based on their specific areas of interest. If you don't know what to give, choose a time-saving gift or service such as gift certificates to local restaurants, a nearby grocery, or even a massage at a local spa. Anything after a long and tiring shift that would be helpful is key. Home-baked meals and goods for the firehouse or police station are good choices when you want to give a group gift. Or, find out what their precinct needs and round up neighborhood contributions to purchase something on their wish list.

Door-Opening Gifts. Live in a high-rise apartment building or condo and have a doorman? Either stick to money or find out his preferences by just asking. Where does he love to shop? What is he saving up for? Consider pooling resources with your entire floor or building and give him a sizable check or gift card or certificate that can be used at multiple shopping locations.

Hairdresser. Hairdressers are deluged with bottles of wine, baked goodies, and traditional gifts. Stand out from the crowd by giving him or her a gift certificate to the swankiest restaurant in town, a piece of silver, shares of his favorite stock, a portable miniature fan for those hot days, or a photo shoot for an updated self-portrait for his publicity features. Or, arrange a group gift and purchase the latest gadget on his wish list. The salon manager can easily help you get the inside scoop on what he really wants!

At Home Helpers. Find out what the baby-sitter, housecleaner, or anyone who helps you out at home wants and loves, that will be the best gift of all. From money to a makeover at your favorite salon, you won't know until you ask. And then add a bonus to thank her for her years of support and dedication. Add a written note that expresses your heartfelt appreciation with artwork from the kids, if applicable.

Marvelous Manicurist. She holds your hands and makes them look perfect whenever you need her, so don't give her the same old thing year after year. Most manicurists get indulged with food gifts and items they don't want and can't use, so give her money or a gift certificate to her favorite store or nearby lunch spot. Make your gift useful and, hands down, that will please her.

Outdoors Lovers. From the latest backpack, sleeping bag, hammock or high-powered telescope for enjoying those summer days and starry nights, there's something for every outdoor lover. Check out the latest camping-equipment store for what's new under the sun, and you're bound to find a mountain of possibilities. Or, if he loves to climb mountains, hike or snow ski, search for gear, clothing, socks, and anything that will keep him warm, cool, climate-controlled, and comfortable.

Gone Fishing. Fishermen have their preferences, so find out if he is a fly, ocean, river, or lake fisherman before purchasing him any fishing accessories or equipment. Is he eyeing a new and improved reel? Or, does he already have everything? Consider giving him a guided fishing trip with all expenses paid for the trip of a lifetime or, at the very least, organize a picnic lunch for his next outing. Add a note that says, "Best wishes for tons of fishes!"

Pet Lovers. A photograph or portrait of someone's pet is the perfect gift for people partial to their pets. Take a snapshot and have it enlarged and framed. Or, have copies made of the pooch or feline and make thank-you notes with the pet's photograph permanently fixed to the front of fold-over cards with matching envelopes. You can also have the photograph printed on a variety of objects including mouse pads and mugs. Add some pet treats to your gift for the purrr-fect present.

Garden Lovers. From a new variety of a rosebush to a pair of colorful garden gloves, gardeners appreciate practical gifts to help their garden flourish. For the gardener who has everything, have a plaque personalized with his or her name for a special touch.

A Stitch in Time. Needlework can take its toll on the eyes. Give your favorite threadmaster a portable magnifying glass to make tiny stitches easier to do. Tell her, "This should help make life 'sew' easy."

A Big Hand. Potters, gardeners, builders, chefs, bowlers, and anyone using their hands a great deal will appreciate a hand from you. Give a gift bag of hand lotions (heavy duty for him), a manicure kit (available in his or hers), or a gift certificate for a manicure, if all else fails. You're bound to receive a big hand in return!

Do-It-Yourselfers. A gift certificate to a home-supply store or local design center will be like heaven on earth for your do-it-yourself enthusiast. Wrap or attach the gift card or certificate around a hammer or to a paintbrush for a handy delivery. Or, check out which tool he's had his eyes on and give it to him with all the gadgets, attachments, or gizmos that enhance it.

A Gift "Fore" You! Give the duffer a treat of golf accessories. Start with a thirty-two-ounce water bottle, and fill it with tees, balls, a cleat cleaner. Wrap a gift certificate to a favorite golf store or catalog around it with a big green bow. Or, consider a golf shirt or that new golf club or perfect putter he's been wanting, but be sure to inquire what the golfer has on his wish list, and you'll score a hole in one. You can also add a certificate for a round of golf at his favorite course. Add a note that says, "Of 'course', we love you!"

Rainy Day Golfer. If your favorite golfer has everything he needs for the game, give him a rainy golf day survival gift. Choose a golf video like *The Legend of Bagger Vance, The Caddy,* or *Happy Gilmore.* Add other rainy-day gifts like *The Worst-Case Scenario Survival Handbook: Golf,* a golf magazine, gift certificate to the pro shop, or a new golf umbrella, if all else fails. You might also include a "to do" list of things that need his attention around the house!

Kitchen Wizard. Be on the lookout for a great new cookbook for a kitchen magician. Or, give her the newest gadget before she has time to discover it for herself. You can also purchase a selection of gourmet spices, herbs, or specialty foods.

Author, Author. If you know an author, it's the little things that count, like registering an inspiring book review online or showing up at his or her book signing with a slew of your book-buying friends. Or, send out an e-mail to all your friends and "cc" the author, recommending his or her new book endorsed by you.

Car Crazy. He loves cars, and loves to tinker. Give him a pair of tickets to the auto show or the next big road race in your area. Add a note saying, "We auto do this together." Or, take a photograph of his beloved possession— his car. But be inventive. Zoom in on the wheel, hubcap, or the license plate, and enlarge and frame it. You're certain to receive an "automatic" thank you for this thoughtful gift.

Find Me a Find. If you have a friend who's a collector, be a second pair of eyes. Check out yard sales, antique stores, and online auctions for incredible bargains and special additions to his or her prized collection. If your friend is an addicted art collector, consider a beautiful coffee-table book or notecards which feature his or her favorite artists.

Working 9-to-5. Anyone who works full-time will appreciate a little help around the house. Offer the gift of a weekly cleaning service for a few months. Add a note that says, "This gift was 'maid' to order for you."

Oceans of Fun. If he's a nautical-goer, devoted swimmer, boat lover, or even a beach bum, give him an SOS gift that fits his passion. From a year's supply of sunscreen to a high-tech pair of binoculars, a barometer, high-powered flashlight, cooler, or additional life jackets, there's something for every sea lover.

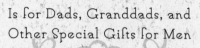
Dads, granddads, and other special men in your life can be a real challenge when it comes to finding the right gift. The good news is that with a little finesse and investigative research, you can score big with any guy on your list.

Forget the wallet and necktie, and go for the gold. Find the one thing he needs, even if he doesn't know it yet. There are many time-honored gifts for that special man, and they're never inappropriate, if well-chosen. Remember, as people age, they don't need "things" as much as attention and service. And love. But first things first when it comes to guys. The gifts in this section are interchangeable. Many items that Dad will love will also suit a Granddad.

Begin by observing his likes and dislikes. Watch the brands he prefers and make sure you know his right size before shopping. Guys don't often have time or affection for shopping and then returning items. If Dad loves to tinker, give him a new addition to his power-tool assortment. If he's an athlete, give him sports equipment. Yes, it's true most guys love those gadgets, but dust collectors are a waste of his time and of your money. So, don't waste a moment and choose a gift that he'll really appreciate almost as much as he appreciates you.

Please note: (See *C* for careers and hobbies for additional gift ideas that relate to specific interest areas and also refer to *Y* for young-at-heart seniors for additional gifts for Grandpa.)

Gifts

Keepsakes for Daddy. Get your kids in the gift-giving habit early. Give Dad a welcome home from work with a gift of art and keepsakes they've created during the day. Make a ceremony of the presentation, and let the kids see how much Dad loves what they do for him. Don't forget to label the art with names and dates for timeless treasures.

The Rules for Giftbuying for Guys:

1. The answers are right before you. Focus on what he does and what he likes. And if he says he doesn't need anything, don't believe him.
2. Check the shirt off his back! Does he prefer collar to collarless or short sleeve to long sleeve? What brands, colors, and styles does he like? Show him choices from a catalog or magazine and see what clothing styles he likes and dislikes.
3. Spy before you buy! Record his sizes, but notice if they change yearly. When in doubt, check it out.
4. Do your homework. Even when you think he has everything, there's always a new putter or gadget available. Just ask his best friends, since they'll either have one or be able to find out and tell you what he really wants.
5. If you don't know his size or preferences, purchase a gift certificate. Guys are famous for taking things back, so make it effortless.

Create a Daddy Book. Give Dad a scrapbook for his birthday so he can save those precious memories and fill the first few pages with poems, pictures, and letters about how and why you love him so much. Each year be in charge of adding cards and photographs to his book. Over the years, the scrapbook will become one of Dad's most prized possessions.

On the Road Again. If Dad travels a lot, send along gifts from the kids. Photos and notes tell Dad he's missed and loved. Hide little "We miss you" gifts like home-baked cookies or self-sticking notes with "I love yous" in his briefcase, luggage, or even his shoes that he'll discover when he's on the road.

A Dozen for Dad. Give Dad a dozen of anything and call it "Daddy's Dozen." Give him a dozen pencils, pairs of socks that he loves, his favorite candy bar, shaving cream, or anything goes. Top off the gift by including a dozen reasons why you love Dad, written on a greeting card or scorecard.

A Daddy-O-Video. Tape Dad's favorite shows while he's at work or traveling, from sporting events to that sitcom he loves. Don't forget to throw in a day or evening of R&R so that he can enjoy your entertaining gift.

Grillin' and Chillin'. Is Dad king of the grill? If so, give him some new grill accessories and fill his freezer with a variety of fixings from steaks to fish and add a card that says, "Chill out and grill out . . . with love from us!" Include a copy of Al Roker's *Big Bad Book of Barbecue.*

Father's Day IOU. Make Dad a coupon book for Father's Day. Offer coupons for cutting the lawn, washing the car, taking out the garbage, doing gardening work, or making simple home repairs, whatever chores Dad normally does around the house. Be sure to include coupons for control of the TV remote on special

days like Super Bowl Sunday and the World Series!

Pay His Dues. Practical dads who belong to a club, gym, golf course, or other dues-paying luxuries might appreciate a year's worth of no dues. Check with Dad first to secure his A-OK and then arrange it directly with the club. Be sure to tell Dad he already paid his dues since he raised you, and now you want to pay his dues for some well-deserved R&R.

Hall-of-Fame Dad. Give the sports enthusiast a framed, autographed photo of his favorite sports hero or moment in sports. Add a note that says, "To our favorite sport!" Or, "To our Hall-of-Fame Dad."

Compliment Jar. Give Dad a jar filled with compliments. Let the kids decorate a jar and add a photo of Dad. Work together to come up with loving things to say to him and write them individually on strips of paper. Fold them, place them in the jar with a note to Dad saying, "Take one a day and smile."

We've Got You Covered. If Dad is a couch potato with a warm heart but cold hands, here's the perfect gift. Give him a big, cozy, chenille throw to keep him warm. Pair it with a pair of fleece-lined slippers and a big mug for his evening coffee.

The Way to a Man's Heart. Let the kids help plan, shop for, and cook a special birthday dinner for Dad or Grandpa. Be sure to chronicle their efforts in pictures to help remind him of his special evening.

"Scent-sational" Gift. Dad probably uses shaving cream, aftershave, and deodorant, but, if he's like most men, there's no coordination in the scents. Buy him bath and shaving products coordinated to his favorite scent, and tell him he's "scent-sational."

Car Fanatics. Nothing is too good for Dad's object of affection: his wheels. Choose a book that chronicles his favorite model, an assembled replica model for his office, a car-magazine subscription, or a certificate for detailing at his favorite "auto spa." The hard-to-please car lover will also love a year's worth of car washes if he's a do-it-yourselfer. Or, how about a yearly subscription to a top auction house's classic-car catalog, so he can dream big?

Words to add:

I'm really sorry . . . it's not a Ferrari!
Miles of smiles on your special day.

We "auto" get together more often. In the race of life, you're a winner.

Your Attention, Please. If you have kids away at college, buy them a calling card with the instruction to use it to make a weekly call to Granddad. He'll appreciate the gift of their attention, and they'll learn that sharing time is important in their busy lives.

Magnetic Personalities. Make refrigerator magnets with your children's photos. Purchase sheets of magnetic material, which you can glue to the back of a photo for an inexpensive, very thoughtful gift. Add a note that says, "Grandpa, we love to hang around with you. Let's always stick together!"

A Lifetime of Learning. If Grandpa's retired, give him the gift of a session at a nearby Elderhostel or for lessons at an activity center. It might just open up a whole new world of education to him. Be sure to include a letter telling him how much he's taught you throughout your life.

Remember When. Find Grandpa a gift of nostalgia. Scour shops for old 78-rpm records, early Pocket Books, and comic books from his youth. Invite him to a party and request that he tell you the story of what it was like when he was a boy. Get out the video recorder or be sure to tape it on audio.

A Novel Idea. If Granddad is a reader, buy him a copy of the latest book by his favorite author, with a note saying, "To a novel father on his birthday."

Rent a Grandkid. If Pop's not able to do heavy lifting anymore, give him the gift of your strength. Tell him he's got the use of your "Rent a Grandkid" service for any moving, lifting, or difficult household chores.

Granddads Are Grand. Have a long-distance granddad? Give the gift of involvement with the little ones. Not just on Grandparents' Day, but all year round. Start a special scrapbook, and once a month send pages filled with photos and drawings to keep him up-to-date on the kids' growing years.

Home Alone. If Papa can't get out much, your company is a thoughtful gift. Bring a picnic or cook dinner for his special day, and bring along a couple of videos to

watch as a family. Your presence is the perfect present.

A Special Gift for Someone Special. Having trouble finding just the right thing for a special man in your life? Give him a fantasy for a day. Invite him to breakfast, and when you pick him up, hand him the keys to his Jaguar or Mercedes rental car for the day. Tell him how he drives you crazy.

Time to Tell. Give that special dad a timepiece. Choose a wristwatch, a stopwatch, or a pocketwatch, with a card saying, "It's time to tell you how much you mean to me." Engrave the back of the watch with "We love you, Dad" and the date for a personalized touch.

This Bud's for You. Flowers aren't just for women. Tell a special male friend you care with a floral gift, accompanied by a note saying, "Hey, Bud, I am so glad our relationship has blossomed."

Proof Positive. Is he a financial wizard? Offer him a proof set of coins from the year of his birth, or a framed silver dollar from that year, with the words, "You're priceless."

Gotta Dance. Some men won't admit they love to dance. And most others are embarrassed to try. Arrange the gift of dance lessons for the two of you. You just might be surprised to find you have a Fred Astaire right under your nose.

Glad About Dad. On his special day, show up at a prearranged time with breakfast in a bag: bagels, Danish, coffee, fruit, perhaps fresh-baked muffins right out of your oven, and a newspaper. Time with you will be the best gift of all.

Traveling Dad. Has he just taken a job where he'll have to travel? Outfit him with a travel kit, complete with battery-powered toothbrush, nail clippers, lint brush, and a travel hairdryer.

For the Mentor. Your success is his reward, too. But let him know how much you appreciate his help. A personalized silver card case or a money clip with his monogram says, "You're a sterling example to us all."

Tied to Perfection. Okay, so you still want to give the man in your life a tie. Give dad an assortment of ties in rainbow colors and tell him he brightens your world. Or, check out the hottest color that's in fashion and update his wardrobe with a stylish selection. Ties are tried-and-true just like your love for Dad, but be sure to add some clever words to jazz up your gift:

Pink tie—"We're tickled pink you're our dad!"

Red tie—"A power tie for our power dad."

Green tie—"Everyone is green with envy because you're our dad."

Striped ties—"Stars and stripes and our dad forever!"

Checked tie—"Dad, thanks for all the checks. . . . Now, here are some for you!"

Polka-dotted tie—"There's a spot reserved in our heart for you."

On a Roll. If Dad travels a great deal or has a bad back, purchase a new luggage set, or even a laptop case, or briefcase on wheels. His back will thank you for it after a long trip.

E
is for Edible Gifts

Perhaps nothing is more indulgent than matching the right food gift with someone's taste buds. Food says, "I care." Food is primal. Food can also be comforting, and it evokes our earliest memories and our strongest pleasures. Face it, we like food. So what better way to give a gift you know will be appreciated and enjoyed?

Gifts of food can be extravagant and wild . . . from Belgian chocolates to truffle oil from France. But it needn't be exotic or expensive to be wonderful. And edible gifts don't need to be entirely homemade. You can add a personal touch to store-bought mixes and end up with a fabulous gift. The secret to giving edible gifts is to first make sure what someone prefers— dark chocolate or milk chocolate? Does he prefer lemon or strawberry? And if he or she has specific dietary needs or is on a diet, think before you bake, buy, and indulge that special someone. Be sure to know before you go shopping for food, fabulous food.

Edible Gifts

A Souper Gift. Layer soup ingredients in a clean glass jar. Start with layers of red, white, green, black, and brown beans. Add dried onions and carrots, dried parsley, garlic, oregano, a dash of salt and pepper. Top with a pretty cover and send a card with the recipe and cooking directions. For an extra special gift, tie a ladle to the jar with a bright ribbon and tell someone she is *souper!*

Coffee Lovers. Coffee drinkers have specific preferences, so be sure to find out exactly what type of coffee he prefers. From caffeinated to decaf, coffee drinkers know what they like. Many coffee stores have special gift cards. Be sure to add a note that says:

Latte lovers: "I love you a-latte," "Thanks a-latte," or "A Latte for my Hot-te!"
Espresso: "I want to 'espresso' my love for you!"

Frappuccino®: "For my favorite chap—here's your favorite frap!"

Decaf coffee: "Til decaf do us part!"

Muffin Mania. Buy prepackaged muffin mix, or make your own. Fill a jar with the mix, cover, and add a small zippered bag of dried fruit for the recipient to fold into the batter before baking. Send packaged with a muffin tin and directions for baking. Add a note that says, "There's muffin like our friendship."

Bowl Me Over. Start with your favorite cereal. Add some toasted oat flakes, nuts, raisins, dates, and brown sugar, all layered neatly in a canning jar. Include a card that says, "Just add milk and love." An extra touch is to send a handmade cereal bowl with a note that says, "You bowl me over."

Mmmmmmmmm Good. One of the easiest gifts in a jar is good old M&M's™. Fill a jar and write a card full of *M* words for the recipient. "You're marvelous, magnificent, magical, majestic, mischievous, matchless, mature, meaningful, memorable, mighty, meritorious, monumental,

and motivational." And that's a mouthful!

Coffee Quickie. Fill a jar with a mixture of instant coffee, non-dairy creamer, a little sugar, and some cinnamon. Add a pair of mugs for an instant coffee break.

For a Lo-cal Pal. If you have a friend who is on a perpetual diet and really appreciates any suggestions or diet tips, fill a basket with diet survival treats. From fresh fruit to vegetables in season, to energy bars and other assorted foods recommended for a dieter, also include a magazine with healthy tips for eating. Or, search the web for recipes that are delicious alternatives and compile them in your own do-it-yourself cookbook with his or her favorite foods in mind.

Confectionately Yours. Flavored sugars are easy to make and fun to use. Stir some cinnamon and a dash of nutmeg into regular white sugar. Put the sugar in a decorative bottle for a wonderfully aromatic gift. Sign your card, "Confectionately yours, [your name]."

Dressing It Up. Make your own salad dressing, mixing good quality olive oil and either balsamic or red wine vinegar, add a dash of your favorite herbs and a touch of salt and pepper. Pour it into a glass cruet with a cover. Deliver to a friend with a head of lettuce, an onion, a tomato, cucumber, and some Greek olives, with your best wishes for a super salad for a super friend.

A Color-Coded Gift. Build a gift of packaged foods in the color of your choice. For example: Tickled pink? (pink marshmallows, candy, cookies, etc.) Feeling blue? (a big blue box filled with candy) In the black? (lots of licorice-flavored gifts) Green with envy? (a big basket of green apples) Shop by color, and you'll be surprised how many items you can pull off the grocery shelves in minutes that are a specific color. From the actual item to the package, it's color-coded and fits the theme. Fill a bag or basket and add a colorful sentiment to top off your gift.

Brownie Magic. Purchase a prepackaged brownie mix and make the batter according to the directions on the box. After greasing the pan, pour in half the batter. Then place two (sixteen-ounce) large chocolate bars (any flavor) across the batter and pour the other half of the batter on top

to cover the bars. Follow directions for baking and then let the brownies cool. Once cooled, place the pan into the refrigerator for fifteen minutes and then slice into squares. The chocolate candy will harden and create a layer of chocolate in the center of the brownies for a sinfully good treat.

A Tisket, a Tasket, a Perfect Picnic Basket. Treat a friend like royalty with a picnic for two. You'll need a basket, paper tablecloth and napkins, plastic plates, and utensils. Fill the basket with a nonperishable feast: pasta salad, cut vegetables, fresh bread and butter, wine, and dessert. Don't forget the candles, matches, and bug repellent.

Exceptionally Good Taste. Help the beginning cook on the way to culinary excellence with a basket of spices and dried herbs, a selection of oils, and a basic cookbook, such as the all-time classic, *The Joy of Cooking*. Send along a note proclaiming, "Your cooking is our pride and joy."

A Taste of Paris. Buy refrigerated crescent rolls. Lay them flat, sprinkle with shaved chocolate or chopped chocolate chips, a bit of sugar, and some chopped nuts, if you like. Roll and bake them according to directions. When you remove them from the oven, drizzle with melted chocolate. Nobody will believe you didn't buy them at that little French bakery across town. Deliver them with a note, "Something edible, for someone incredible."

Easy and Elegant. Purchase good quality dried apricots, and dark and white chocolate bars. Melt the chocolates separately, and carefully, in the microwave. Dip one end of each apricot into one of the chocolates and lay on a sheet of waxed paper to dry. Arrange the dried fruit pieces in a gift tin, chocolate side up, for a gift that's as pretty as it is tasty.

Fruit of the Vine. For a fruitful relationship, when giving assorted fruit include a note that says, "Assorted wishes for a happy holiday." Choose juicy peaches: "You're a peach of a friend." Oranges: "Orange you glad we're friends." Cherries: "Life is just a bowl of cherries when I'm around you." Pears: "We make a perfect pair." Pineapple: "Aloha friend." Blueberries: "I'm blue without you."

Soup's On. If you're sick, what sounds better than homemade chicken soup? If you don't make your own from scratch, open a few cans, add some vegetables, noodles, and shredded chicken for a friend who's under the weather. Add a copy of *Chicken Soup for the Soul* by Mark Victor Hansen and Jack Canfield, and you have a perfect gift for whatever ails them.

Just Sweets and Desserts

Calling all Cookies. Cookies are one of life's little pleasures. Home-baked cookies are always a sweet treat, and if you don't have time, there are endless choices to grab at the grocery store or corner bakery. Here are some clever deliveries and catchy captions to accompany them.

Any type of cookie: "To the smartest cookie I know!"

Animal cookies: "Congratulations to a party animal!"

Chocolate cookies: "I'm 'choc' full of love for you."

Chocolate chip cookie: "To a chip off the ole block."

Chocolate mint cookie: "We were 'mint' for each other," or "We were mint to be friends."

Fortune cookie: "No message needed. You are my fortune!"

(Replace the fortune with this one.)

Fudge cookie: "My love for you and fudge will never budge."

Lemon cookie: "Sorry I was sour."

Sugar cookie: "Sugar and spice—you're everything nice."

Oatmeal and raisin: "Oatmeal and raisin for your special occasion."

Peanut butter cookie: "I'm stuck on you."

Sandwich cookie: "You fill my life with love."

Thumbprint cookie: "Thumbody loves you."

Wedding cookies: "You two are smart cookies to have found each other."

Cookie Kisses. Buy prepared cookie dough from the supermarket. After cutting the dough, press a chocolate kiss into the middle of each cookie. Follow the directions on the package for baking them and once totally cooled, put them in a doily-lined tin for giving, and add a note, "Kisses and cookies just for you"

Gifts That Keep Coming and Coming. You've heard of the clubs that send you books, or fruit, or cakes, or plants each month. Do it yourself and tailor your gift to the recipient's exact taste. Send a card telling what he'll be getting and when. If her birthday is on the seventh day of the month, perhaps arrive on the seventh of every month. You can do it once a month for a year, on special holidays, or as an annual birthday treat.

You Take the Cake. Cakes are a wonderful gift to give, and the secret to making it a perfect gift is to add words that will ice your gift and top it off with your special finishing touch.

For cakes of any kind add these words: "You're the icing on the cake," "You take the cake," or "Thanks for making this job a piece of cake!"

Angel Food cake: "To an angel of a friend."

Cheesecake: "A big thanks to the big cheese. Say cheese and enjoy this gift!"

Chocolate Chip cake: "Chip, chip—hooray!"

Strawberry cake: "I love you 'berry' much."

Special Delivery. Give a cake (store-bought for the hurried shopper or home-baked for the baker) on a beautiful cake plate and add a note that says:

This cake and plate are
especially for you,
To thank you for all
the sweet things you do.
I hope this gift brings
lasting pleasure,
And reminds you—you're a
friend I treasure.

A Blast from the Past. Find out what candy your gift recipient enjoyed as a kid and recreate a gift filled with this blast from the past. With these gifts you're bound to get an earful when you inquire about a favorite childhood candy and then give it in abundance. Be sure to add words to sweeten up your gift even more!

Bubble gum: "I sure know how to 'chews' friends."

Candy corn: "I know it's corny, but I really love you."

Fire balls: "I've got the hots for you!"

Lemon heads: "When life gives you lemons, call me!"

Lifesavers: "You're a real life saver." Or, "We're on a roll."

Lollipops: "Popping in with birthday wishes."

Red hots: "With love from your red-hot lover."

Sticky candy or stick of gum: "Thanks for sticking with me."

Sugarfree candy: "You're so sweet, this candy didn't even need sugar!"

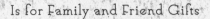
Family and friends are our favorite gift recipients. They can be the most fun to find gifts for, but they can also be the hardest, too. Expectations often run high, and time to find the ideal gift can be short. Smart giftgivers keep a gift journal, detailing what you give each person close to you for each holiday, and plan ahead.

Since we give family and friends more personal items, you'll want to note sizes, color, and style preferences. It's a huge help to record any details that will help steer you toward the right gift. And while you want to make your gifts special and a surprise, you might want to compare notes with others who will be giving gifts to the same person to avoid undue duplication.

Sundaes on Sunday. If your family has lots of kids, give them a perpetual ice cream party. Purchase an electric ice cream maker or arrive (announced, of course) with all the ice cream and top-

pings. Bring sprinkles, nuts, whipped cream, cherries, and extra gooey toppings and syrups.

A Book of Wishes. Honor a family member's special occasion . . . a graduation or engagement perhaps, with the entire family's best wishes. Have everyone write his best wish for the honoree on beautiful paper you distribute ahead of time. Take a family photo to serve as the book's cover, and have it bound at a quick-copy store for a love-filled keepsake to treasure.

Say It with Song. Can't sing a note? Ask a friend who sings really well to call your favorite someone and sing a song that expresses happy birthday, good luck on the job, or I'll miss you. Give him or her a little script, and you'll be surprised how much it will mean that you took the time to arrange this.

Ties That Bind. Do you have an older child going off to school and leaving a younger sibling behind? Cement the friendship with matching jewelry, a bracelet for girls, matching dog tags for boys. Have them inscribed, "Friends forever" with both names and the date. Let the older child send the memento to the younger one after a few day's absence, with a note that says, "If you ever need me, call me!"

Mission Possible. Make it your mission to celebrate important family holidays with an elderly or infirm relative. Your presence is the best present you can give. Bring the kids and take lots of photos to send later, bound in a simple scrapbook. Include a magnifying glass and card that says, "It's clear to see how much we love you!"

I Relish You. Let a special friend or family member know they are relished. Fill a basket with condiments and relishes to spice things up. Add a sentimental note expressing how you relish him or her and include pickled relishes and sensational salsas for a mouth-watering gift. If she's one hot mamma, select plenty of hot sauce.

The Blues. If you are apart from a friend or family on a special occasion, send them the blues. From a blues CD, to a blue sweater, or even just a jar filled with blue M&M's™, you get the idea. Add a poem:

*Roses are red, but I'm feeling blue.
It's your special day, and I'm
thinking of you!*

Home Movies. Organize your photo albums, your stacks of unsorted pictures, and your home movies for a very special family gift. Have a video service transfer all your pictures and films onto videotape or DVDs. You can make copies for holiday gifts for everyone, and place a copy in the safety deposit box for safekeeping, too.

"Cell-a-bration." Give your teenager a cell phone for a special "cell-a-bration." A cell phone keeps her in touch and gives the teen a way to stay connected with you for starters. Set the ringer to the music of choice, and late at night hide it next to her bed. Call her number before her alarm goes off to wake her up with a big surprise.

A "Tree-mendous" Farewell. Is a dear friend moving away? Make a gift he or she will really cherish . . . a friendship tree. Draw a tree, and label each branch with the name of a friend. Include addresses and phone numbers, spouses' and children's names and birthdays. It will not only be a keepsake, but a valuable resource for keeping in touch as well. Invite the friends whose names you've inscribed on the tree to add a "leaf," a note telling how much the friendship means, how the departing person will be missed. Send it to your friend's new home with the comment, "We will miss you tree-mendously."

Shake It Up, Baby! Have a friend on a diet? If she thinks she's looking her age, losing her youthful glow, or feeling blue, give her something to glow about. Wake up her body and her spirits with your personal attention from the gift of an exercise class you take together, or a pre-scheduled weekly walk.

For a "Scent-sitive" Friend. Brighten a special friend's day and give her a large candle with a gift certificate for services at her favorite salon. For a clever delivery, wrap the certificate around the candle with a bow tied to hold it in place. Tell her she's beautiful inside and out, and thank her for her ongoing scent-sitivity. Select a yummy scent from chocolate to cinnamon that you know she'll love.

Happy Thoughts. You don't need a special occasion to make a friend feel better. Give a box of smiles filled with happy thoughts like, "You're not getting older, you're getting better," "Somebody loves you," and other famous quotes, song lyrics, and inspirational sayings designed to lift spirits. Write them on strips of paper, put them in a box decorated with smiley faces, and send with instructions that read, "Take one smile a day."

Focus on Friendship. Here's a creative spin you can use for any occasion. Begin by selecting and giving a gift that represents each letter of the word you've selected. For example, you want to celebrate your friend. For the letter *F*, choose flowers. For *R*, a ring, *I* for ice cream, and so on through the word's letters. This idea works for any occasion, or you could even try this with the person's first name, or a word like *forty*, *love*, or *happy*.

Five-Star Friend. For a spectacular friend who deserves a five-star rating, take her to a five-star restaurant for a meal she'll never forget. During the meal, present her with five stars and write why she's so special on each one. Have the waiter bring one of the stars out with each course or refill.

Is Fashion Her Passion? For a stylish career person, give the latest hot accessory . . . perhaps for him a tie in that new color and, for her, whatever is totally trendy and in style, ranging from the must-have ruffled romantic shirt to that to-die-for vintage purse. A working girl would also appreciate a stylish business-card holder with a famous logo or her initials front-row center. Add a subscription to a favorite magazine that focuses on design trends for a year-round gift filled with fashionable advice.

Salt of the Earth. Give a beautifully packaged basket or box of indulgent bath salts and tell your friend she's the salt of the earth.

Give Her a Hand. Offer a friend who is busy or infirm an extra pair of hands or feet. On index cards, make up coupons for chores they can't easily handle, such as babysitting, grocery shopping, a trip to the bank, a home-cooked dinner. Put the coupons in a pretty recipe box and write on the outside, "Call us for our presence. We're standing by!" This would

be a welcome gift from a group of friends in times of stress or of bereavement, too. Be sure to add telephone numbers to make it easy to redeem each person's good deed.

It's in the Cards. The avid card-game player who loves a good hand of gin rummy and solitaire always appreciates a good "deal." Find decks of playing cards that combine this passion with another interest. If your friend collects some nostalgic memorabilia, send that theme. There are cards for just about every hobby, from pets to flowers.

The Perfect Deal. Make up a care package with chips, a dip mix, beverages, and cards. Include tallies for bridge players and chips for poker types.

Words to add:

"Nature dealt a perfect hand when she created you."
"You're better than a royal flush."
"Partner, you're seven no-trump, doubled and redoubled."
"I'm betting on our friendship."
"In my book, you hold all the aces!"
"When you count your friends, deal me in."

A Book with Heart. When in doubt, give a book. A favorite suggestion is *When I Loved Myself*

Enough, by Kim McMillen and Alison McMillen (St. Martin's Press, 2001), about how to make the most of every day and take care of what's really important in life. This book is filled with jewels of inspiration that a special friend or family member will treasure.

To a Jewel of a Friend. Thank a special friend for being a priceless jewel in your life by selecting a beautiful piece of jewelry. Notice first if she prefers yellow gold, white gold, or silver; if she prefers traditional items or handmade creations by artisans. Add a note that says, "To a gem (or jewel) of a friend. I value you more than words can say."

Roadside Assistance. If you have a favorite teen who is newly licensed, or a friend or family member who travels a lot or is always on the road, consider a year's membership to an auto-service club. The emergency road service is a real lifesaver in case of a flat tire or an engine glitch.

Listen My Children and You Shall Hear. One of the best gifts an older person can give her family is the gift of history. Keep a portable tape recorder nearby and gradually tell your story, and the family's history, as an oral record to pass down through the generations. If you have access to a video recorder, that's even better.

The Real Deal. Brighten a friend's day with a deck of playing cards, a tally sheet, and a note, "You're the real deal."

Family Focus. Add an original touch to a family gathering. Place one-time-use cameras on the table and ask everyone to take pictures throughout the party. Have the pictures developed and make up albums for the attendees.

Breakfast Surprise. Celebrate friends and family with a specially prepared gala breakfast gift. Call the night before to make sure you know what time to deliver your A.M. surprise. Pack a gift bag with fresh fruit, croissants, juicy jellies, and add a note that tells them they are "a peach of a relative."

Going Places. If someone you know is going to far-off places, give a flat expandable tote bag that can be packed on the outbound trip, then filled with laundry or souvenirs if the luggage gets overfilled during the vacation.

A Shining Light. Have a friend who brightens your day? Give her a flashlight or key chain with a light on it, and add the note that says, "You brighten my world."

Soap-Opera Diva. Do you have a friend hooked on the afternoon soaps? Give her a journal to write down *her* thoughts and aspirations. Inscribe it, "These are the days of our lives" or "To my bold and beautiful friend."

You Are My Sunshine. Brighten a low mood for a friend with a suncatcher, a small stained-glass figure to hang in a window. Match her décor, or give a heart or a sun, with the hope that it will lighten her load when the sun shines through.

G

Is for Get-Well Gifts and Expressions of Sorrow

Nobody enjoys being sick, so we all do our best to help out . . . to make our sick or injured friends feel better, both physically and mentally. A friendly face or voice is a big help, but you can't be there every minute. So consider choosing gifts that stick around and make a difference. Brightening someone's day is a meaningful deed and a get-well gift can mean so much to someone who is ill.

Expressing your sympathy is also one of life's most challenging gift-giving dilemmas. Often those you wish to comfort just aren't ready for words or company. However, when you express your heartfelt feelings, they are treasured forever. Gifts that ease the pain, comfort the mourning, and honor the departed are most meaningful. Here are some examples that will get you started helping to heal those you care about.

Get-Well Gifts

A Little "Tea-L-C." Fill a teapot, bag, or basket with assorted teas and honey. Add a note that says, "Here's a little tea-l-c!"

Lean on Me. If someone you know is to be confined to bed for a long period, offer an extra shoulder . . . a bed pillow for sitting up in bed with good back support. Some even have pockets to hold tissues, eyeglasses, or the TV remote. Include a note that says, "Be sure to lean on me and this gift, too."

Pop-up Soon. Give a tin of popcorn or assorted bags of popcorn in a colorful popcorn bowl. Add a note that says, "Hope you'll pop-up soon."

All Right Soon. Give a selection of writing pens and stationery in a pretty box. Add a note that says,

"Hope you're feeling all 'write' soon!"

Hey, Mr. Postman. Lying in a hospital room can really get boring. Help a friend look forward to the daily delivery of mail by sending a card each a day during a hospital stay. Choose cheerful cards with hopeful sentiments, or make up your own like, "Every day that you're sick, I hope will go by super quick!"

Get-Well Goodies. Check out the grocery store to see what fruit is in season. Fill a basket with a healthy selection and add a note like the following:

Assortment of fruit: "Assorted wishes for your quick recovery."
Pears: "Hope to 'pear' up with you soon. Get well quick."
Apples: "An apple a day didn't keep the doctor away, but we're thinking of you right to the core!"
Oranges: "Orange you feeling better yet?"
Peaches: "Hope you're feeling peachy keen soon."

A Puzzling Present. Nothing whiles away long hours in bed like puzzles. Offer a bag full of cross-word puzzles, word finds, plus a clipboard for support, and a cross-word dictionary. Say, "It's no puzzle why we all love you! Get well soon!"

Back in Bed. If it's a bad back that's the problem, give the comfort of an updated heating pad with all the bells and whistles. Include a card saying, "Hope you're *back* in the saddle soon."

Cast Away. If someone you know has a broken arm or leg with a clunky cast, help make the best of it. Bring a set of markers in bright colors, and creatively autograph the cast. If the friend is a child, bring a bag of stickers for friends to help decorate (and redecorate) the cast. Include some other activities to entertain him by assembling a "First Aid Fun Kit" filled with games, little toys, and penny-candy treats.

Once Upon a Time. It's so hard to keep a sick child engaged. Bring a fairy tale and basket of stuffed animals that resemble the characters in the book. The child will enjoy acting out the parts of the book with the various characters.

Super Hero. Wish a child or someone who is young at heart a speedy recovery with a selection of superhero-themed comic books.

Add a note that says, "We'll all feel *super* if you get well soon!"

Back on the Road Again. If someone you know has ongoing back problems after being in bed, give him an auto back massager. It fits over the car seat and offers both heat and massage, easing the strain on his back while he's driving. Include a note that says, "Hope you're 'back' to normal soon."

On Call. When there's a patient in the house, everyone's on constant alert. Take a bit of the stress away with your gift of a two-way monitor. One end goes in the patient's room, the other wherever the caretaker is, so no call or problem will go unanswered. Or, give a bell so the patient can ring, ring, ring if in need.

Fountain of Love. Offer a diversion for the bed-bound friend. How about a tranquil fountain with water softly cascading down stones into a pool? There are small electric fountains available that need only be plugged in and filled with water to provide a soothing background whisper of sound.

Laughter Is the Best Medicine. Help your favorite patient take her mind off her illness with a selection of humorous videos. Rent them from a local videostore, and exchange for fresh ones every few days. Go for slapstick like the Marx Brothers or contemporary comedians like Chevy Chase or Steve Martin. Add a note that says, "We'll be all smiles when you feel better!"

A New View. Give the child who's stuck in bed a kaleidoscope. Its constantly shifting patterns can provide hours of enjoyment. You might want to include a book about kaleidoscopes, or even a kit to build a simple one.

No Bored Games. If the patient hates being confined, help pass the time with a gift of board games. There are games for everyone from the young preschooler to the adult. Add a note that says, "Enjoy these bore-dom busters and get back in the game soon!"

It's in the Cards. Card games help pass the time if you're sick or injured. You can give regular decks of cards or popular card games like Old Maid. Include a note, "You'd better get well soon. Don't forget who you're dealing with."

Music to My Ears. For someone who is hospitalized, choose an inexpensive handheld CD player and a selection of music CDs as your gift for the patient. Or, send a music box or a favorite CD with a note that says, "Your recovery will be music to my ears."

Ahhh Spa. Know a young girl who's under the weather? Grab her interest with a basket of cosmetics and goodies like bright nail polish in wild, shiny colors, eye shadows, blush, and lipstick for her to experiment with while she's recuperating. Add a mirror so she can see what she's doing, and a one-time-use camera to record the results.

Basket Case. If you know someone who's a basket case from the prospect of being in bed, give her a basket full of small treasures to help pass the time and make life a bit easier. A nail file, a mirror, reading glasses, and a good book, a TV guide, a bottle of water, a pack of gum or mints, a package of tissues, and—last but not least—chocolate.

The Smell of Success. Did you know that ancient people used aromas to heal? Today's aro-matherapy scents are so wonderful, it would be a great idea to share some with a recovering friend. Let a professional help you choose appropriate products, and give them with the thought, "To the sweet smell of your successful recovery!"

All Scream for Ice Cream. Ice cream is a favorite treat when someone doesn't feel good, so arrive with some frozen pleasures and stock up the freezer. Include a variety of toppings for your freezer-pleaser.

Don't Worry, Be Happy. If a friend is in bed and can't do much with his or her hands, give a set of handsome worry beads. Rubbing them between the fingers is a very relaxing sensation. Add a note that says, "Don't worry, be happy soon!"

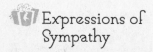 Expressions of Sympathy

Words from the Heart. Words from the heart enter the heart, and expressing your sympathy in writing immediately helps. So, when you hear someone has died, write a condolence letter to the family and deliver it as soon as possible. Share what the deceased meant to you and, in the event you didn't know him or her, reflect upon their accomplishments you've learned about through others or in the obituary. Personalize your letter in a heartfelt way and deliver it as soon as possible, offering your words of comfort.

Angel on My Shoulder. If angels are important to your grieving friend, give a flock of them: a pin to wear, a statue to display, a framed print, and a pretty book featuring angels. Add these words, "Your guardian angel is watching over you in this difficult time, and so am I."

In Memoriam. Help the world remember the departed by making a donation in his or her memory to a cause that was important to him or her during life. Give to a school, church, synagogue, or charitable organization that mattered to him. Make sure a gift card will be sent in your name to the family, but also send a condolence card as well and mention how you are thinking of them and have made a contribution. This is especially meaningful since you are letting the grieving know your thoughts are with them. Whenever possible, pay your respects with a visit to the family and offer your condolences in person as well.

Search for a Cure. If your friend's death was due to an illness as yet uncured, make a donation toward finding a cure. Look in the phonebook, or call your local medical association for direction. Write a letter to the individual sharing your hope and contribution to finding a cure.

Memories. While some people hesitate to talk about the departed, most mourners deeply appreciate the chance. Make up a memory book with your fondest memories of him or her, including photos if you have any, stories of good times spent together, your reflections on their great qualities. Offer it with your love and sympathy, and the offer of a willing ear whenever the mourner wants to talk.

Don't Forget. When a departed parent, sibling, or friend's birthday or anniversary comes around, give the gift of remembrance. If one of your parents has died, the living parent still has the anniversary. Send a card or flowers. Say, "Happy Anniversary. You were so lucky to have had Dad for forty-five years. We are thinking of you and him, today and always." Or, remember the person's birthday with a contribution or card sent to the family saying how much you miss him, too. They'll appreciate your thoughts beyond words.

Cook Ahead. Help out the mourners with a gift of dinners. Do this one yourself or organize a group to plan meals for a week or two. Prepare freezable foods like casseroles in disposable containers. Wrap well, label with contents and reheating directions, and stock their freezer. Send canned vegetables and other nonperishables, too. Be sure your note identifies all the contributors, "Prepared with love from your friends."

Trace the Family. While the family is together and in mourning, create a family tree. Complete as much as possible, then let family members assist you and fill in the blanks. When it's done make a copy for each family member and write something special by each deceased

person's name to honor their life and importance to the family. Over the years, update the tree and share it with future generations.

A Token of Love. There are many objects that have a special meaning to the family of the deceased, but perhaps you have a photograph or item that belonged to the person that you could share. Make a copy of the picture and place it in a frame. Or, choose something meaningful like a wind chime that would play music in the family garden to remind them of the beautiful soul of the deceased person. You could also select a special music box that plays a song the deceased loved, but there are endless ideas. The key is to add your heartfelt feelings in writing along with the gift about why you're giving this gift and what you hope it will accomplish.

Is for Holiday Gifts

The holidays are a time when your gift-giving skills are really put to the test. The challenge is clear. So many gifts and so little time! What's a shopper to do?

The key to keeping your sanity during the holidays is to make sure you carefully plan your gift list. Be in the know before you go shopping, and you'll be better equipped to deal with both friends and family. Research what they really want. With a little preparation and thought, you can sail through the holidays and make giftgiving a cinch.

While the holidays are rich with traditions, it's important to find out what holiday your recipient celebrates in the event you do not know in order to ensure your gift is on time and in good taste. Christmas is the season of Jesus' birth. Religious rituals commingle with secular festivities in the year's biggest joyous occasion. Hanukkah, the Festival of Lights, commemorates the miracle of one day's worth of sanctified oil lasting eight days as Jews fought to save their religion. Kwanzaa is a modern holiday that celebrates the African American people, their culture, families, and history. It lasts from December 26 through January 1.

And one final thought to help you navigate holiday giftgiving: Smart giftgivers know that when they stock up on gift items that fit many individuals on their list, they save time, money, and loads of energy. From an indulgent fruit company that offers the juciest oranges on earth, to an inspiring book, to a great gadget that's easy to use and is cost-effective, it's always a good idea to have a few holiday favorites as well as resources on hand that are guaranteed to please!

(*Please note*: Refer to *S* which is for special days and occasions for additional holiday gift suggestions.)

Deck the Halls. Give an organizer or a clear storage box filled with wrapping paper and all the odds and ends for giftgiving. When you hit the big sales at the mall, stock up on clearance Christmas cards, decorations, and ornaments. They're likely to be deeply discounted, and the money you save will be a great start toward next year's giftbuying. Add a note that says, "You're a gift to us all!" Or, create a rhyme like either of these:

Jingle bells, jingle bells, thanks for all you do!
We're giving you the wrapping, since our favorite gift is you!

Deck the halls with boughs of holly, Here's a gift to make you jolly!

All the Trimmings. If Christmas trees are part of your family's tradition, start early with a lovely tradition of your own. Give each family member an ornament every year, with his or her name and the year inscribed. For your kids, buy duplicates and put one set safely away. When your child is grown and setting up his or her own household, give the duplicate set for the first Christmas. For a meaningful idea, photograph the ornaments every year and create holiday-photo greeting cards.

Teacher's Choice. Instead of giving that special teacher another plate of cookies or a good ole mug, give her the gift of choice: a gift certificate to a nearby restaurant, gift card to her favorite mall, tickets to the movies, or something practical she will really use and enjoy.

***C* is for Christmas.** Add the fun back to Christmas giftgiving and take the word *Christmas* and give a gift that begins with each letter in the word. *C* might be for candles, candy, or cash. *H* is for a heart-shaped piece of jewelry. *R* is for anything red. You get the picture! This is a fun tradition for everyone to follow when filling stockings, too, and a great way to add a little challenge or pizzazz to Christmas giftgiving.

Away from the Manger. If a loved one has to be away for the holiday season, send him a little bit of home. Ask each family member to make a small contribution. Some decorations, a box of Grandma's cookies, a pine-scented candle, and a framed photo of those left behind, with a card full of love and kisses, "Christmas isn't complete without you. Hurry home, we miss you."

Seasons Gr-eatings. Nothing makes a kitchen smell more like Christmas than baking gingerbread. Let the kids help you make gingerbread men as special gifts for friends' children. Send your recipe, a gingerbread-man cookie cutter, a big gingerbread man, and a copy of the children's classic book, *The Gingerbread Man.* Your card can read like a line from the story, "Run, run as fast as you can. You can't catch me, I'm the Gingerbread Man."

Sock It to Him. Everyone enjoys socks, and here's a clever spin on the customary Christmas stocking. Indulge him with a pair of designer socks or a luxurious pair made from cashmere. He'll be the first to step up and say thank you! Add a note that says, "No one can fill your shoes! Merry Christmas."

Mint for You. Give a cheery sweet gift of mints. Find a pretty glass jar and alternately layer red- and green-wrapped peppermints for a pretty presentation. The kids will enjoy helping you make these. Add a bow and you're ready to go!

Make a Memory. Have a self-sticking nameplate engraved and attach it to a scrapbook for a special gift. For example, it could read "The Johnson's Christmas 200—" for a personalized way to save the memories. This gift will be enjoyed for years to come and is an extremely thoughtful and useful present.

Stocking Gifts. Each year deliver a stocking to a shelter for the homeless and load it with goodies. Make the stocking out of felt and ribbon, or buy one. Fill it with oranges, nuts, candy, and some basic essentials like toothpaste and a new toothbrush. This is wonderful to do each year as a tradition during the holidays.

Baby's First Christmas. Let the grandparents share in the joy of baby's first Christmas. Take a picture ahead of time, with baby in all his or her Christmas finery. Most photo shops, online photo stores, or copy centers can transfer the photograph to calendars or an entire array of products just in time for Christmas giftgiving.

Hanukkah

A Gift of Lights. Hanukkah is the Festival of Lights. Let your gift reflect that and purchase gifts that brighten people's homes and their lives. From colorful frames in every color of the rainbow, to a new desk lamp, to flashlights, to silver candlesticks and colorful candles, there's something for everyone. Add a card, "May the lights of Hanukkah shine bright in your heart."

Do You Know the Latke Man? Latkes are potato pancakes, fried in oil, another symbol of the holiday. Pack up a box of latke mix, an egg, an onion, and a bottle of vegetable oil, and offer it as a special Hanukkah gift with your family recipe. Or, make someone who doesn't cook homemade applesauce to top off ready-made latkes.

Dreidel, Dreidel. A dreidel is a four-sided spinning top, a game traditionally played on Hanukkah. Make up gift bags for children. Include a dreidel, a handful of pennies for betting, and a bag of Hanukkah gelt, chocolate coins covered in gold foil. This is also a wonderful collection to start for a child, and there are endless choices. Every Hanukkah give a different kind, from clay to hand-blown glass to china or wood. Write out the verse from the traditional song on your gift card, "I have a little dreidel, I made it out of clay. And when it's dry and ready, then dreidel I shall play."

A College Care Package. If a loved child is spending his or her first holiday season away from home, make sure it's not without a menorah and candles, a dreidl and some gelt. Pack these essentials up with some homemade cookies shaped like Stars of David and menorahs, decorated with blue sugar crystals.

Chocolate Symbols. Give a box of homemade Hanukkah candies, and you'll get a huge smile in return. You can buy plastic molds of dreidels, menorahs, and six-pointed stars at most craft-and-hobby stores, along with blue-and-white and chocolate candy-coated wafers. Melt the wafers over hot water and spoon them into the molds. Refrigerate a few minutes to harden. Turn the mold over; the candies should fall right out. Put them in a gift box or on a doily on a platter for a most-admired gift.

Grandma's Cookies. Take a hint from my grandma Annie Freedman, who taught me how to bake her memorable chocolate chip cookies. Her family-honored tradition was lovingly called "Grandma Freedman's Cookies," but her secret recipe can be found on the Nestle Toll House Cookie™ chocolate morsel bag.

Synagogue Gift Shops. The perfect resource for gifts for Hanukkah can be found at local synagogue gift shops, as well as Judaica stores that specialize in Jewish gifts. From menorahs in all shapes and sizes to challah covers and beautiful mezuzahs, there are endless choices available to commemorate the holiday.

The Eight Nights of Hanukkah. Here's a wonderful tradition to make giftgiving special during Hanukkah: A special theme is assigned to each night and gifts are exchanged with that focus in mind. From book night to game night to T-shirt night, the choice is yours. To add a meaningful twist, consider the first or eighth night for giftgiving to others who are less fortunate.

All in the Family. When you don't know what to give each member of a family, consider giving the entire family a "together" gift. Choose something the entire family will enjoy, like tickets to a special show or sporting event, a new television with a DVD and VCR player built-in, a contribution for that computer they want, games

they can play, an ice cream or smoothie maker, or something the entire family will enjoy together.

Kwanzaa

Read All About It. For the novice, there are several books to explain Kwanzaa to friends. For children, give *Let's Celebrate Kwanzaa*, by Helen Davis-Thompson. It's full of activities for kids three-to-ten years old. *Kwanzaa: Everything You Always Wanted to Know But Didn't Know Where to Ask*, by Cedric McClester, explains the seven basic principles of the holiday along with customs and suggestions.

The Festival of the Harvest. Fruits and vegetables, the results of the harvest, are an integral part of the Kwanzaa celebration. Give friends a basket generously filled with beautiful ripe mangoes, bananas, peaches, oranges, plantains, and other family favorites.

A Kwanzaa Symbol. Offer as your gift a Mkeka, a mat woven of paper, fabric, or—preferably—grass or raffia. This mat is the base that holds all the other Kwanzaa symbols, and it symbolizes the experiences, culture, achievements, and sacrifices of African ancestors.

An Enriching Gift. Kwanzaa also focuses on self-improvement and enrichment. Choose a gift that is educational or highly creative like a craft book or a book all about nature crafts that the entire family can enjoy. Creativity is a key focus during Kwanzaa, and this would be a welcomed gift during this artistic celebration of African American values.

I

Is for I'm So . . . Gifts

I'm so happy, excited, apologetic, bothered, concerned, delighted, elated, glad, proud, sorry, tardy, or filled with joy! When you have emotions to express, but you don't have just the right words, there are many creative ways to find just the right gift to express your sentiments.

From "forgive me" gifts to "yahoo for you!" presents, and everything in between, a little thought and a little thoughtfulness will make the moment memorable and get your point across. Just be sincere, be yourself, and go for it!

Saying "I'm Sorry"

Pour on the Apologies. If you simply bothered someone and want to apologize, give a bottle of Tabasco sauce with a note that says, "If you're not still hot and bothered, how about dinner soon? I promise to pour on the apologies. I'm sorry!"

In the Doghouse. Find a stuffed dog with a totally sad expression. Send it with a note saying, "Dog gone-it. I barked up the wrong tree. Forgive me!"

Put Out the Fire. If you've really made someone mad, send a fire extinguisher with the note, "I know you're really burned up at me, but can't we put out the fire soon?" Or, "Sorry, I was one hot mamma!"

Nuts About You. If your irrational actions upset someone, send a bag of nuts and a nutcracker. "I know I acted nutty. I am nuts about you. Please forgive me!"

Sorry I Blew It. You lost it, you got so upset and blew your cork. Send a bottle of champagne and say, "I know I blew my cork. Please forgive me." Or, a bouquet of balloons will help you rise to the occasion and admit you blew it!

Common "Cents." OK. You really messed up. Go to the bank and get a dollar's worth of shiny new pennies. Put them in a gift box, wrap it up, and include a note that says, "I'll use some common cents next time. Sorry!"

Let's Make Up. Take the first step toward soothing hurt feelings. Give her a tube of her favorite lipstick or shade, or makeup and a compact with a note, "Let's kiss and make up." If you've had a spat with a guy, send him a bag of candy kisses and tell him, "There's an apology in every kiss."

The "Write" Touch. So you did it, you really hurt somebody. But you don't know how to say, "I'm sorry." Express your feelings and specifically admit what you did that was wrong in writing and ask for forgiveness. Verbally reinforce your apology by stating it in person, too, face-to-face.

Time to Get Over It. Have you and a friend been squabbling? Don't know how to take the first step toward reconciliation? Send a windup alarm clock and say, "Isn't it time we let this argument wind down?"

Start Over. Say you're sorry with a bouquet of pencils and a note saying, "Can I erase the mistakes I've made and begin again?"

Lost Your Cool? If you lost your cool, say so, with a pint of ice cream or anything that's ice cold. Add a note that says, "Sorry, I lost my cool."

 I'm So Proud of You!

Your Biggest Fans. A portable desk fan from his or her fan club will keep her cool and feeling appreciated. Add a note that says, "With love from your biggest fans."

On a Roll. Give any designated amount of rolled coins from pennies to quarters. Add a note that says, "Congratulations, you're on a roll!"

I'm "Sew" Proud. When you are really proud of someone, give a small sewing kit with the note, "I'm sew proud of you, I'm busting at the seams."

How Sweet It Is. Send an assortment of sweets or duplicates of one favorite candy with a note that says, "To your success. How sweet it is, and how proud of you we are!"

Thanks for Being There. She was a buddy when you most needed support. Buy a bottle of her favorite perfume and send it with a card, "Your support at this difficult time was heaven-scent."

Proudly Loudly. Say how proud you are in front of all her friends by presenting her with a good ole blue ribbon for being your first-prized wife. Have a waiter secretly surprise her while dining with friends. Or, tell her you're proud by sending an orchid in bloom with a note of congratulations for her "blooming" success.

Movin' on Up. For a promotion at work, give a kitchen step stool or a stepladder. Say, "I am so proud of you for working your way up the ladder."

A Fruitful Friendship. Say hello to a faraway friend with a crate of oranges and a note, "Orange you glad we're friends?"

Color Me Ecstatic. Make up a basket of colored pencils, crayons, markers, or anything colorful (such as ribbons, T-shirts, or socks) for someone who's had a major personal accomplishment. Add your thought, "Color me ecstatic at all you've accomplished!"

I'm So Lonely—I Miss You!

There Aren't Enough Words. Send a dictionary along with a card, "There aren't enough words to express how much I miss you."

I'm So Blue Without You. If a friend is faraway, let her know how much you miss her with a box of anything blue. From stationery, pens, a scarf, to a note written on blue paper and in blue ink saying, "I'm so blue without you."

I Can't Bear Being Without You. Buy a cuddly teddy bear for someone moving away. Tell them, "I can't bear the thought of being without you."

A Picture Is Worth a Thousand Words. Away from a loved one? Send him or her a note and include a photograph of yourself holding a sign that says, "I miss you! Picture us together soon!" This is also perfect for a grandparent, sibling, or anyone you really miss.

J

Is for Jewelry, Gem, and Birthstone Gifts

All that glitters: engagement rings, wedding rings, fraternity pins, friendship rings. Jewelry is a universal symbol of love, affection, and achievement. It runs the gamut from gumball-machine plastic to stainless steel, sterling, gold and platinum; from glass to diamonds and everything in between. A hint: When you purchase jewelry, be sure you are buying from a reputable source, one whose merchandise you can trust. Nobody wants to pay for rubies set in gold and end up with cut glass in base metal that turns your finger green. When buying gems, look for pure, deep color, without clouds or inclusions, chips, or cracks. Make sure settings are tight. And make sure you can return or exchange what you buy, in case you select the wrong gift.

Beyond its beauty and inherent worth, jewelry speaks its own language. By adding heartfelt words and your deepest feelings, jewelry can also become a timeless treasure far beyond its actual worth. Here are some ideas and suggestions for selecting gems that will express your affection and make those you care about feel very special.

January's Jewel. Give your favorite January birthday a deep red garnet. Add a note that says, "Garnets are red, but I'm feeling blue, Whenever we're not together, I'll be thinking of you."

February's Gem. February's child celebrates with the purple amethyst for sincerity. When giving one add a note that says, "This amethyst reflects the honesty and sincerity in your eyes and your smile."

Sky-High in March. The color of March is pale blue with a beautiful aquamarine. Be sure to tell her your love is deep as the blue ocean or high as the sky.

Showers of Diamonds for April. Tell her diamonds reflect her flaw-

Month-by-Month

MONTH	COLOR	STONE
January	dark red	garnet
February	purple	amethyst
March	pale blue-green	aquamarine
April	white (clear)	diamond
May	bright green	emerald
June	cream	pearl or moonstone
July	red	ruby
August	pale green	peridot
September	deep blue	sapphire
October	variegated	opal or tourmaline
November	yellow	topaz or citrine
December	sky blue	turquoise or blue topaz

less character. Tell him diamonds are forever, and so is he. Comment on the many facets of your relationship. Diamonds are a girl's best friend and are a lasting way to say, "I love you."

Hope for May Flowers. May's gem is the deep green of the emerald, signifying eternal hope. Include it with a copy of *The Wizard of Oz* and add a note that says, "You are my emerald city." Or, "Home sweet home is sweeter because of you."

June's Bride, in Pearls. The lustrous gleam of June's gem comes from pearls, the symbol of health and vitality. Be sure to include a note that says, "In the sea of life, you're my pearl."

July's Ruby Red. The most famous red gem is July's ruby birthstone. It promises contentment for those who wear it. "Only rubies can express the burning red flame of my love for you."

August Jewels. August's color is pale green and represented by the peridot, a beautiful green stone. Tell her, "Everyone will be green with envy because you are my jewel."

September's Sapphire. Sapphires signify repentance, but make it clear you offer them out of hope and love. "The sapphire's blue depths echo the depth of my feelings for you."

October, *O is for Opal*. Opals mean love and variety. "Our love is unique and fragile and, like I cherish you, I hope you will cherish this gift."

November's Fire Shines. Offer the beauty of November's yellow topaz with a note that says it means cheerfulness. Add a note that says, "I hope this topaz will make you as happy as you have made me."

Turquoise in December. December's birthstone is the handsome blue turquoise, the symbol of unselfishness. Add a note that says, "When you're around, the only thing that's blue is this gem!"

Gifts of Jewelry

Lock It In. Love someone special? Show your affection with a dainty heart-shaped locket. Don't forget to put in your picture! Write, "You know I love you. I just wanted to lock-et in your mind how much."

Namely You. "Brand" your name on a friend's heart with an engraved friendship bracelet. "Glad we linked up as friends."

Friendship Circle. Say "Be my friend" with a shiny circle pin. "Like the circle in this pin, our wonderful friendship has no end."

You're Number One. Tell someone just how special they are with a "#1" pin or pendant. It can say #1 Mom, #1 Dad, #1 Grandma, #1 Grandpa, #1 Teacher, #1 Friend, or just plain #1. Include a note that tells him or her why!

From Mother to Your Significant Other. When you give a gift to your special someone that was your mother's or grandmother's, such as jewelry or a family treasure, include a note that says, "This is going from the first woman I ever loved to the last woman I will ever love."

Stuck on You. Scour the antique shops for a fancy vintage stickpin and give it with a note, "Thanks for sticking with me."

A Ringing Endorsement. Show someone how much you care with a star sapphire ring or the gemstone of your choice. "Here's a ringing endorsement for my love for you."

Eye of a Tiger. Tiger's eye is a distinctive brown-and-gold stone. Make your feelings known, "I've been 'eyeing' you for a long time."

Off the Cuff. Give him a knockout pair of cuff links and a French-cuff shirt, saying, "Off the cuff, I think you're great."

A Hip Clip. What to give the man who has everything? How about a gold money clip engraved with his initials? Add a note that says, "A hip clip from your favorite chick."

Ring Around the Toesies. If she's really crazy for jewelry, give her a toe ring and a pair of sandals so she can show it off. "Ring around a rosie, here's something for your toesie." Also, add an ankle bracelet for that well-dressed soul.

With This Ring I Promise. Include a special song when you give her that ring. Check out The Platters' "With This Ring I Promise" or Stevie Wonder's "I Just Called to Say I Love You." Make sure it's playing in the background when you give her the gift. Arrange ahead of time at the restaurant with the piano player or hire a violinist to appear and play a romantic song like "As Time Goes By." Or, pop your song into your CD player in your car, set it to play when you turn on the engine, and pop the question under a starlit sky and a silvery moon.

Formal Attire. To commemorate a special black-tie event, present him with a set of studs for his dress shirt. Add a note that says, "To my favorite stud."

Confucious Says. In the language of gems, the Chinese consider jade a good luck charm, a symbol of love, virtue, and status. Jade is often paired with gold in a carved good luck charm, a great gift for someone starting out on a new adventure or career. Everyone will be green with envy over this gift.

A Clear Choice. Jewelry needn't be gold and gems. Give a necklace of brightly colored glass or clear synthetic stones which are inexpensive. Tell her, "It's 'clear' how much I love you!"

A Pearl of a Gift. Delight any woman with an elegant strand of pearls. Choose dainty ones for little girls and classic larger pearls for the ladies. All you have to tell her is she is a pearl of a girl. When you purchase them, check with the jeweler for other options for future special occasions. Next time, you could give her a special diamond clasp or pearl enhancer.

Watch Out! He'll never forget the time thanks to his elegant antique pocket watch, complete with fob and chain. Have it engraved with a special code you create like, "ILY" (I love you) or "IAHTFY" (I'll always have time for you!).

Time Out. If you've been too busy lately, find her a lovely watch. From a casual sports watch to one that's perfect for evening, give it to her with a card saying, "Let's make more time for each other."

In the Mood. Tell your loved one you're interested with the gift of a mood ring. It changes color as her mood changes. Say, "I'm always in the mood for you."

It's Sacred. For a very special occasion, choose a religious symbol, if you know it will be appreciated and worn. A crucifix or cross, a Star of David or mezuzah, an ankh, whatever spiritual symbol fits the person and his or her beliefs. Present it with a note, "My life is blessed thanks to you."

Bedazzled. Make the gift of jewelry fun. If a friend is creative, offer a box full of specially chosen beads, wire, a needle for stringing, and a selection of clasps. Add an instruction book on jewelrymaking for the do-it-yourselfers.

Works Like a Charm. Make a special occasion even more memorable by finding just the right charm to add to a special bracelet or to her collection of charms. Tell her she's charming, or sign your gift to the Belle of the Ball from her Prince Charming.

Just Name It. Thrill a friend with a name necklace, a gold necklace with her first name in gold letters. You can find these in English, Hebrew, Greek, Arabic, Cyrillic, Japanese, and Chinese. Tell her, "What's in a name? A rose by any other name would still not be as sweet as you." Or, "Your name is embedded in my heart."

All Eyes on This Gift. Does she wear glasses for reading? Is she always losing them? Find her a pretty jeweled holder to clip onto her glasses. You can find beads, real pearls, even funky modern styles.

Momma's Got a Brand New Bag.
Choose a whimsical jeweled evening bag. Go from silver or gold-mail designs, to needlepoint, to stunning boxes covered in gems. The choices are limitless, and so will be her gratitude for this unique accessory.

All Ears. What lady wouldn't like a pair of earrings to complement her clothes, hair, and her pretty face? If she's already got stud earrings, buy her several pair of drops, attachments that hang down and change the look of her old earrings. Or, when in doubt, give hearts: silver, gold, diamond, or platinum. They all make a perfect gift.

Sparkle SOS. Help her keep her jewelry sparkling with a battery-powered sonic jewelry cleaner.

Don't forget to add a refill of cleaning solution and the necessary batteries. Tell her she adds a sparkle to your life, or she's a sparkling success!

Treasure Chest. When you're buying jewelry, don't forget a place to store those treasures. Don't bury them, but keep them safe and handy in a velvet- or satin-lined jewel box. Add a note that says, "Rings on your fingers and hoops in your ears. This box will keep your treasures safe through the years."

Keep It Safe. If she's been accumulating "important" jewelry, even if it's just important to her, give her a fireproof closet vault to keep her valuables safe from intruders, fire, and her own forgetfulness.

K

Is for Kids—Toddler to Teen Gifts

It is such a pleasure to give gifts that really please children. For them, every day is an adventure and every gift is a treasure and opportunity for fun. Let your imagination run as wild as theirs, knowing that they can find pleasure in the smallest kindness, even the box your gift came wrapped in. It's always best to let a child make a wish list and then inquire what his heart is set on. If your budget doesn't allow for that high-tech pricey gadget, it's always best to be honest ahead of time. If you intended to find a specific gift but couldn't locate it, consider giving a rain check, but always keep your gift promises.

The good news, however, is that gifts for kids come in all shapes, sizes, and prices. They can range from art supplies to collectible dolls and books or games. Choose durable, safe, age-appropriate items, and you'll earn a child's thanks and a parent's gratitude. When in doubt, pack-age a gift certificate or gift card inside an inexpensive trinket and add some pizzazz to your presentation.

Plus, don't limit kids' gifts to established holidays. Make your own occasions: first day of school, half-birthdays, trips to the beach. Celebrate a new sibling, a new tooth, a trip to the doctor. And keep in mind that your presence is the best present. Your time is the best gift of all: a day at a theme park, a trip to the zoo, a movie, or a picnic in the park. (A *note*: Parents like gifts of clothes, but some kids see that as a disappointment, so check first. On the other hand, most teenage girls think clothes are the ultimate gift!)

The following gifts are arranged from younger to older and are excellent suggestions for nieces and nephews, grandkids, godchildren, your kids, and your friends' kids, too.

(*Please note*: See *B* for additional birthday gifts for kids and *M* for gifts for newborns.)

Reading Greetings. Instill a love of reading from the beginning. Whenever you give your toddler a toy, try and include a related book about the object. Reinforce the concept that reading is fun and raise a reader from the very start. For example, combine a stuffed Pooh bear with the book about Winnie The Pooh. Add a note that says, "Oh Pooh, this is for you!"

Baby and Me. When a new baby arrives, make sure big brother or big sister is part of the fun. Give the older child a one-time-use camera to take pictures of the baby. Help make a scrapbook of his or her photos. Make it clear that this is his or her gift to the baby, and that he or she can share it with their friends at school and in the entire neighborhood.

Blanket Buddies. Most toddlers have a "blankie," a beloved object they carry constantly, sleep with, and won't be without. When your child finally relinquishes his security blanket, have it cleaned and repaired, put it safely away, and save it to give when he's grown, perhaps when his first child arrives. Take a picture of it to create a memory to be cherished.

First Haircut. Make it a gala occasion. Give your child a new stuffed animal to take to the hairdresser or barber, a companion to show there's nothing to be afraid of. Save a few locks of hair with a tiny bow around it in a keepsake box, and capture the moment with a photo and send it to the doting grandparents.

My Big Bed. Celebrate a child's moving from crib to bed with the gift of a "bed buddy," a stuffed animal or doll that stays in bed with him. Be sure to tuck the buddy in, too, and make nighttime a fun time to wind down and enjoy his or her big boy or girl bed.

First Day of School. Make the first day extra special with a special gift: a book bag or tote bag filled with pencils, markers, paper, and colorful school accessories. Tell her you are sending it filled with love, just for her.

My First Set of Wheels. A first bike is a huge occasion and calls for lots of picture taking. Let your child help pick out the bike and a helmet, and make sure it fits his body comfortably. When the big day arrives, give him his helmet and a sheet of stickers to decorate it. Be sure he understands never to ride without the helmet, and be there to guide him safely to bike-riding success.

Are We There Yet? Make long automobile trips a pleasure with a cargo gift bag. Agree ahead of time when the gifts will be given: each morning, after lunch, each evening. Find things that will make the time go faster, such as card games, books, word-search puzzles, and colored pencils with paper. Bring along a separate bag for each child, or fill a shoe bag and hang it over the back of the driver's seat with incentives for cooperation along the way.

The Tooth Fairy. Give your child a special Tooth Fairy pillow, one you can make from a small throw pillow. Decorate it with dental floss and a toothbrush, and add a small pocket for the tooth and, of course, the reward from the Tooth Fairy. Personalize the child's name on the pillow with a marker or fabric paint.

Scout's Promise. When your youngster joins the Boy Scouts or Girl Scouts, surprise him or her with a "ditty bag," a canvas bag with the basic gear needed for that first camping trip. Include a canteen, metal plate, collapsible cup, all with the Scout emblem.

Half-Birthdays. Make each family's half-birthday special by having your child help bake and decorate a half-birthday cake. Bake a cake and cut it in half (save the other half for later or bring it to Grandma). Decorate it with "Hap Birt" for a fun family tradition.

The Old Ball Game. Make a big deal out of your family's first trip to the baseball stadium by giving your child his own junior-size baseball glove to help him remember watching the "big league" play.

Numerically Speaking. Help your child learn the concept of numbers with gifts to count. Give him a set of eight crayons, three tennis balls or two roller skates, with a big card with the number drawn on it, and lines to lay out and count the items.

Spelling Bee. When she learns to spell her name, give her a bag of gifts starting with each letter. If her name is Ali, give her an Accessory, a Locket or Lollipop, and an Ice cream store gift certificate. Kids also love to pick out the gifts, and this can be done at the grocer with snack-food items and candy as well.

Sorry You're Moooooooving. If a favorite child is leaving town, give him a stuffed cow and include a card saying, "Sorry you're moooooving away. We'll miss you!"

I'll Be Baaaaaaack Soon. If you have to go away, tell your child you'll be back soon with a cuddly lamb to keep her company. Tell her, "I've got to go away, but I'll be baaaaaaaack soon."

Pamper the Camper. Purchase an inexpensive toy football or rubber ball, and cut a slice in it. Fill it with goodies that will surprise your camper. If the camp allows it, you can also fill a piñata for an added gift the entire cabin will enjoy.

Princess Charming. If a favorite little girl is invited to take part in an adult situation, like a graduation party or a wedding, give her a charm bracelet ahead of time with a charm geared to the occasion.

Tell her, "This gift will remind you to be your charming self today."

Just Say, "Thanks." Encourage your kids to write thank-you notes with a gift of personalized cards. Make them age-appropriate (clowns or bunnies for youngsters, funky flowers or sports themes for young teens, and more formalized notes for older teens). Include stamps and an address book with relatives' and friends' addresses already entered. Include the helpful book, *The Thank You Book for Kids: Hundreds of Creative, Cool and Clever Ways to Say Thank You*, by Ali Lauren Spizman. (www.thankyoukids.com)

The Sweetest Kid on Earth. If you've witnessed your child do something particularly nice for another person, give her something sweet, and include a note that says, "To the sweetest kid on earth."

Teen Talk. Give your teen (or 'tween) the gift of private communication with friends: a phone of her own with a private line so she can stay in touch. If you really want to go overboard, include telephone features like call-waiting. Select a telephone that is also an answering machine. Can't miss those special calls!

Concert or Theater Tickets.

I know you love music,
so here's a surprise.
A gift to delight both your
ears and your eyes.
A music CD to enjoy
right away,
And tickets for you on
the concert's day.

A Cd for You from Me. When your child brings home a great report card, when he scores the winning goal, when she studies hard for a tough test, give a gift card for a CD or DVD. These random gifts are a great bonus.

Music to His Ears. If your teen has been working extra hard at school, on exams, SAT's, science projects, give him a pair of tickets to a local concert and a gift certificate for dinner for him and a friend. Or, give a gift card or certificate to his favorite music store.

Still Daddy's Little Girl. When she's ready to go off to her first dance, Daddy can give her a necklace with a pearl pendant, reminding her that she'll always be Daddy's little girl.

Hot Wheels. If your teen's car is the center of his life, give him a book of coupons for car washes and oil changes. Add a personalized key chain, or bucket and supplies for him to do it himself.

Personal Necessities. When a teen is heading off to college, help get her started with a gift bucket of bathroom necessities: soap with a plastic holder, toothbrush and toothpaste, shampoo, lotions, and a pair of towels with his or her initials embroidered on them.

A-OK Résumé. Give him a gift that offers a jump-start in life. Help him organize a résumé of his accomplishments and work experience, and update it yearly. Begin this when he is in the ninth grade in high school and keep a running résumé that will be useful for both college applications as well as part-time jobs. When he graduates college, he'll be ready to go and look like a pro. E-mail him a copy to update over time, and help him get ready for success.

Phone Home. Graduates will appreciate prepaid calling cards for those excessive calls to friends across the country. Add a note that says, "Wherever you may roam, don't forget to phone home!"

Also, include an erasable message board for those VIP messages from home.

Safe and Sound. Give the gift of safety gadgets that add extra protection: a fire detector and a carbon monoxide detector with a lesson on how to install them. Encourage him to check out his dorm rooms or apartments for working safety devices and fire escapes. Tell him to be sure to put your gift to work for extra peace of mind.

We-Care Package. The best care package includes a little of this and a little of that. Send a pantry pleaser filled with favorite snacks from your cupboard that your college student loves. Bake some fresh chocolate chip cookies and load him up with duplicates of his favorite basics from toothpaste to shampoo, the latest best seller, and some extra quarters for the laundry. Add colorful artwork from younger siblings and funny pictures of the entire family to put a smile on his face.

On a Roll. The best luggage for a college student or traveling teen is a large duffle bag on wheels that's easy to store while at school. Have one monogrammed and throw in some personalized luggage tags for a can't miss gift!

Candid Camera. A videocamera is an excellent gift for any teen interested in making home movies, pursuing a related career, or just capturing life as he or she knows it. Check out the options for at-home editing and consider a gift that is a life-long hobby, talent, and skill.

Shop Till You Drop. Give your teenager a few shopping coupons to visit stores of her choice, when she wants to go. Create your own redeemable coupons and offer your chauffeur services for two hours of shopping (or however much you can manage) with advance notice and your mutual consent. Be sure to include your undivided attention and total patience!

Teen-Approved Books. It's often tough to be a teen, so select some books that will inspire the teen on your gift list. Here are a few that have stood the test of time and have the seal of approval from other teens: *Teens Can Make It Happen: Nine Steps for Success* by Stedman Graham, and *Chicken Soup for the Teenage Soul: 101 Stories of Life, Love and Learning* by Jack Canfield and Mark Victor Hansen.

Indulgent Gifts. Older teens and young adults love those indulgent gifts that adults enjoy: massages, manicures and pedicures, facials, and heavenly body treatments. Find a spa nearby and treat her to a half-day of beauty, or him to a reflexology session or a hot stone or sports massage. Throw in some fabulous skin-care products or top-of-the-line shaving creams and body lotions to crown your present. Oh, the thanks you'll receive for this gift!

L

Is for Last-Minute Gifts

Oops. The party's tonight! His birthday is tomorrow! You've forgotten their anniversary . . . again. What to do? Like many, you're singing the last-minute blues. Not to worry! There's always a creative answer to your dilemma. A little work, a dash of inspiration, and you've got it made.

Gifted givers know that in order to always be prepared for those thoughtful gifts, you must have an assortment of gifts on hand or, at the very least, gift ideas and resources at your fingertips. Every giftgiver needs a few favorite 1-800 numbers, online shopping sources, and dependable contacts who can help out in a flash. In the back of this book you'll find a section to record your gift-giving contacts that are standing by 24/7, so be sure to list your favorites for those gift-giving emergencies. In the meanwhile, here are some gift ideas for those last-minute shoppers who procrastinate or for giftgivers who wish to give gifts which look like they've stayed up all night contemplating.

Stock a Gift Closet. The very smartest way to be prepared for last-minute gift emergencies is to keep a well-stocked gift closet with a variety of selections. Pick up bargains and generic gift items whenever you see them on sale. Keep an assortment of colorful gift bags, toys, favorite best-selling books, handsome pens, gift cards to video stores, homemade goodies in the freezer, and a few hot CD's from favorite performers for those last-minute gifts. Then, when you need a gift, just reach in the closet and, *voila*, you're good to go!

Grab It and Go. Here's a minute-made gift that you can grab at the grocery or drug store. Give a magazine tied up neatly with a brightly colored bow or put it in a gift bag from the store. Remove the subscription card, fill it out, and send it in as soon as possible. Include a card that says, "Have no fear, your gift will be here . . . (monthly, that is, with love from me!)

Phone Home. Stop by almost any store, even a gas station, and you can purchase a phone card. It's perfect for the traveler, college student, or anyone with friends and family in other cities.

Funny Money. Give a gift of cash and even inflate it! Roll up the cash and put it into an inflated balloon tied on a ribbon. Add a card, "Break the balloon and you will see, a gift inside for you from me."

Can't Top This! Fill a bag with ice cream toppings including chopped walnuts, mini–chocolate chips, M&Ms™, and chocolate and butterscotch syrup. Pick up a container of ice cream and drop it by their house with a card that says, "A friend like you can't be topped!"

Snack Attack. Fill a gift bag with soft drinks, chips, nuts, and cookies from the grocery store for a last-minute gift a teen will appreciate. It's a perfect gift for studying around the clock.

Shopping Spree. Here's one way to deliver a belated gift. Creatively announce he or she is getting a shopping spree on you. E-mail or send a belated card that says, "I know I'm late—but call me ASAP, to schedule your gift—It's a shopping spree!"

Recipe for Success. Copy some favorite and easy recipes on colorful index cards. If you don't have a recipe box for them, attach and send them with a card, "Wishing you a big helping of happiness on your birthday!"

A Perfect Pair. An instant anniversary gift for friends is to fill a gift bag or basket with juicy pears. Add a note that says, "Happy Anniversary to a perfect pair."

A Gift of Time. Make up an instant gift certificate promising your time for one day to be used as the recipient wishes, or you can specify a day working in the garden, shopping, helping do spring cleaning, errands, whatever. "This coupon is redeemable for one day of my undivided attention."

Encourage-Mint. Fill a clean jar with mints, and add some words on a note filled with encouraging inspiration. Tell your friend to, "Take one every time you need a little encourage-mint." Or, if someone entertains you, add a note that says, "Thanks for the entertain-mint!"

Birthday Factoids. If you're stuck for time and fresh out of ideas for a birthday present, go to the Internet and find a site that tells interesting things about his or her birthday. What celebrities share it in common? What other famous people were born that day? Print out the information on a colorful piece of paper, roll it up, and add a bow to give an informative gift.

Ornamentally Yours. Here's a challenge. On the day after Christmas, brave the mobs at the mall and scoop up all the Christmas ornaments you can find at bargain prices, and stock up for next year. You'll be ready to top off every gift with an ornament or give a tree-full at a fraction of the cost.

Dinner for Two. What does a smart cookie make for dinner? Answer: reservations! Do it. Call a knockout "in" restaurant and make reservations for two. Call and reserve an evening for a last-minute gift with all the trimmings.

Gifts on the Net. If you really don't have time to shop, get online and find a virtual gift certificate. You can print it out in seconds for a ready-made present anyone will appreciate. Follow it up with an e-mail that says, "With this certificate, you can buy 'virtually' anything!"

Dinner's on Me. You're a gourmet cook, but you don't have the time to whip up a culinary creation. Offer a gift certificate, good for one home-cooked dinner, complete with candles and wine, for a date to be agreed upon in the coming weeks or months. Add a note that says, "Bon appetit . . . dinner's on me!"

Movie Review. Swing by the videostore and purchase gift cards for several movie rentals. Add a box of microwave popcorn, a box of candy, and a couple of soft drinks. Add a note that says, "Lights! Camera! Your re-Action! Hope you enjoy this gift!"

I'm Rooting for You. Take cuttings from houseplants and start them rooting. You never know when you'll want to put some soil in a pot, add a plant and a bow, and send it to a new home. "I'm rooting for you!"

Oops . . . Miss a Special Occasion? If you missed the big one, pick up the phone and call your local florist. Some can offer same-day delivery, complete with a card from you. Add a card that says, "I'm a blooming idiot to have forgotten your birthday! Forgive me. Hope it was happy!"

Cool Tools. There are countless pocket-sized tools on the market that have loads of gadgets, all in one. Similar to a pocketknife, the all-in-one novelty will include a pair of miniature scissors, screwdriver, bottle opener, and many other functions. Locate a few to have on hand from your local hardware store and remember the Boy Scout motto: Always be prepared!

Mirror, Mirror. When you don't know what to get a teenager or woman of any age, purchase a magnifying mirror. From compact-sized to vanity styles, it's a useful gift and easy to find when last-minute shopping.

Pleaser Freezer. The freezer is the ideal place to store edible gifts that can be frozen and thawed out in a jiffy. From cheesecakes to fancy breads and home-baked sweets, the freezer is one place that will keep your gifts until you need them.

M

Is for Mothers, Grandmothers,
New Moms, and Baby Gifts

From mothers to grand-mothers, new moms to baby gifts, there are endless ideas for memorable giftgiving. The arrival of a new baby is one of the most exciting gift-giving opportunities. There's so much to be done, so much anticipation! And once the baby's here, it all begins again, with congratulations, gifts, and planning for the future. Not to mention sleepless nights, tons of diapers, and planning for college . . . enough to exhaust the best of us.

And while we're talking about new moms and babies, let's not forget the moms whose babies are older, or grown with babies of their own. Moms are very special people and deserve the very best. There are many ways to let her know with a gift just how unique and important she is, and the ideas in this section will hopefully assist you in accomplishing your goals.

The Rules for Buying Gifts for Women

1. Don't guess. Observe her favorite colors, brands, places she shops, and find out if there is an item she has her heart set on.

2. Add words to your gift that make her feel special. Women love to feel appreciated, and this will be the finishing touch to make your gift more meaningful and memorable.

3. Be in the know before you go shopping. Avoid anything she dislikes, including perfumes if she's allergic, scents if she is sensitive to smells, and fattening foods if she is on a diet.

4. Occasionally, surprise her with a gift when she least expects it. On a special occasion, however, never wait until the last minute.

5. Choose a gift that reflects her interests. Consider giving her something she collects or is

interested in. She will appreciate that you cared and noticed!

Moms

Mom's Day Off. Pick a day and give her the royal treatment. Throw in a construction-paper or plastic crown (or tiara) and give her a day off. Take over the chores, and give her a book, a candle, and a box of her favorite candy to indulge herself and relax. Order in dinner and rent a movie she'll love. Add a note that says, "Mother's work is never done, but today's your day to have some fun!"

Glued Together. After a trying time, give mom a basket of useful desk accessories, personalized note pads, and a bottle of glue with a note, "Mom, you're the glue that holds this family together. Also include tape, paper clips, a stapler, and other things Mom needs to keep it all together.

Share How You Care. Once in a while, when she least expects it, on no special day in particular, send Mom a pretty nosegay of flowers in a rainbow of colors. It's a perfect fit for her desk, nightstand, or bathroom vanity. Tell her how her presence brightens your life.

Good Scents. Give Mom a bottle of her favorite perfume with a note saying, "You taught us the importance of good scents. Now, here's some for you!"

How Does Your Garden Grow? Does Mom love her garden? Pick a spring day and have everyone in the family show up for a day of garden work. Tell each person to bring a plant or bush to beautify the yard. Give Mom a glass of lemonade and a folding chair so she can sit and direct the crew.

Crazy for You. Do you drive your mom crazy sometimes? Let her know you're aware of it. Send her a big bag of cashews, walnuts, peanut brittle, or her favorite nutty snacks, with a note that says, "I know I drive you nuts. Thanks for loving me no matter what!"

Treasured Recipes. Don't let her lose those precious family recipes. Give her a blank journal and a supply of pens for her to transcribe her favorite heirloom recipes and kitchen tips. Or, surprise her, and transfer all the recipes yourself.

Mom's Got Mail. If Mom's afraid of technology and has a brand-new computer, give her an introductory course on how to use it. At the very least, make sure she's e-mail savvy to stay in touch with family and friends online. If she doesn't have a computer, consider an e-mail-only gadget that lets her send and receive such messages.

Mom's Cup Runneth Over. Give Mom an addition to her china: a fine bone china cup and saucer, a new or antique tea service, or a set of coffee mugs with the note, "Because of your love, our cup runneth over." If her pattern is out of production, take a photograph of it and check local antique fairs and stores that specialize in out-of-stock china patterns.

A Perfect Day. One of my favorite gifts of all time was when my husband and kids gave me a perfect day. I got to choose everything everyone did all day, from cleaning the garage to going shopping with me. This gift of choice plus everyone's undivided attention and total cooperation was pure heaven.

Time to Tell. Give Mom a new watch with a big, easy-to-read dial, and tell her, "It's about time we told you that we appreciate you in a great big way."

A Very Important Date. Help Mom remember important family dates like birthdays and anniversaries with a book of days. Record for her each family member's birthday, along with sizes, preferences, and addresses. Add a picture of each individual for a special touch.

Mother's Nature. If Mom's nature is to write notes on the back of grocery receipts or torn pieces of newspapers, give her a supply of personalized notepads. Have them personalized with "From the desk of [her name]," or, for a mom with young children, "From the Mother of Jake and Emma." Check into self-sticking notepads as well as personalized papers of all shapes and sizes. Also order a few self-sticking address labels for a time-saving gift.

Serenade in Blue. Do something she'd never expect. On a special occasion, hire a violinist or guitar player to serenade Mom under her window, in her living room, or at a restaurant while lunching with friends. Send along a big bouquet of flowers and tell her the gift is from "her biggest admirers."

For a Spa-tacular Mom. Is Mom feeling a little stressed out these days? If so, be sure to *stress* how much you love her and give her a little R&R. Purchase a selection of services at a nearby spa and add a note that tells why she's so *spatacular*!

Mother-in-law. Give her a necklace with a heart inscribed "Best Mom." Tell her, "I am so lucky to call you Mom."

 Grandmothers

(*Please note*: See *Y* is for Young At Heart for more options for grandparents.)

For a Charming Grandma. Celebrate Grandma's special day with a gift from the whole family. Give her a gold chain with hearts for each of her children and grandchildren. Have the charms inscribed with each person's name or initials, or inset with each one's birthstone. Tell her, "You are a precious jewel to us all."

Memories for Grandma. Create a memory book for Grandma on Mother's Day. Ask all her children and grandchildren to write a note with their fondest memories of Grandma and why they love her. Bind them in a pretty scrapbook

along with photos taken through the years with the family, and present it as a treasured keepsake.

Easy Reader. Give Grandma a telephone with large numbers she can easily read without her glasses on, or check to see if her favorite magazine subscription is available in a larger type. These are many supersized ways to tell her you love her in a great big way. If she wears magnifiers and is always losing her glasses, check out her glasses, the specific number (which will range from 1.0 to 3.0), and purchase assorted colors in her favorite styles with eyeglass holders for easy locating.

Always in Stock. If Grandma appreciates practical gifts, give her items that she likes to stock up on, from stamps to tuna fish to her favorite brand of paper towels. Give her a month's or longer supply of the item and save her time, money, and energy.

Magnify Your Love. Is Grandma hard of hearing or seeing? Give her a magnifying make-up mirror for those tired eyes. Or, consider other gadgets that make life easier, like hard-of-hearing telephones with volume controls for magnifying the sound so Grandma can hear you ring.

The Gift of Choice. Gift cards and certificates are tried and true, but still the ideal gift of choice for any grandmother, especially those who want nothing and have everything. From restaurants, to favorite places she loves to shop, to local bookstores, reflect her shopping habits and local places she frequents. Or, choose a bank credit or gift card and load it up for that special trip she's always wanted.

New Moms

New Baby 101. Check out leading baby-care books like those from pediatrician T. Berry Brazelton to keep new moms informed with helpful tips. Include a colorful bookmark with your telephone number written on it, offering to baby-sit just in case she needs a break.

R&R for Mom. Start Mom off with a first-aid kit just for her: a parenting book for those "what to do now" emergencies, a pouch of herbal teabags, a heating pad for her aching back, and a freezer filled with delicious homemade soups and quick meals when there's no time to cook.

Rock-a-Bye Baby. One of the most thoughtful gifts you can give the new mom is a rocking chair. Its gentle motion lulls baby to sleep and relaxes a worn-out mom or dad. Your card could read, "Rock-a-bye baby, in the treetop. This gift is for those nights when the crying won't stop!"

Close at Hand. Provide the new parents with help close at hand. Find a pouch to fit over the arm of the chair, to hold a cordless phone, and fill it with necessities: a small flashlight, a magazine, and a towel for middle-of-the-night messes.

Tools of the Trade. Help Dad make the most of his part in baby's first months. Give him a workman's toolbelt filled with cotton balls, baby wipes, diaper-rash cream, baby powder, baby oil, baby shampoo, and a clothespin for his nose. Tell him, "Congrats on your new job."

Mama's Got a Brand New Bag. Help the new mom juggle baby's paraphernalia with a brand-new microfiber, washable diaper bag. Include some baby essentials like wipes, disposable diapers, and tissues for the mom on the go.

Rub-a-Dub-Dub. Purchase an open plastic-handled box or basket. Fill it with cotton balls, disposable diapers, baby shampoo, baby oil, baby wipes, an instant-read thermometer, diaper-rash ointment, baby powder, baby body wash, some baby washcloths, towels, and don't forget a rubber ducky! With paint, personalize it for "Baby's First Bath."

Bragging Rights. Don't forget Mom and Dad will need a supply of small photo holders and frames ranging from purse size to photo key chains, and refrigerator magnets to show off baby's photos. Send some to the new grandparents as well. Give them an assorted supply with a card, "We're all smiles since [baby's name] arrived."

Not a Creature Was Stirring. But if he does stir, Mom will hear him with your thoughtful gift of a baby monitor, so she can get some rest in her own room while baby sleeps. This is a must-have gift for all new parents.

Start a Tradition. When the baby is born, give Mom a birthstone necklace, a chain containing a photo of the baby with its birth-

stone inset and its initial inscribed. As more babies arrive, Mom can count on more baby charms for her necklace.

 For Baby

Memory Box. One of my favorite gifts that I picked out when our daughter Ali was born was a beautiful heart-shaped wooden box. I called it "Ali's Memory Box" and lined it with satin. Sixteen years later, it is now filled with Ali's baby rattle, a silver spoon, her baby bracelet, and other treasured gifts and remembrances from the first year of her life.

A Gift That Will Register. Just like they did for their wedding gifts, inquire if the new parents now registered their wish list for their baby. If so, find out the correct spelling of the couple's name and the baby's due date, and check with the store the parents registered at. There are so many items a new baby can enjoy, so choose a gift they selected and is at the top of their wish list.

Snuggle Up. A baby carrier that holds baby close as Mom or Dad shops, does housework, goes for a walk, or just relaxes is a most thoughtful gift. Be sure to look for one that holds baby securely but comfortably for both baby and parent. Add a note that says, "This gift will help keep your most precious possession close to your heart."

Counting Sheep. Give a goodnight gift by combining a soft, plush lamb with a book of rhymes that includes "Baa Baa Black Sheep." Add a note that says, "Sweet dreams!"

Baby Steps. Choose baby's first pair of shoes, and with them give a gift certificate to have the shoes bronzed or encased in porcelain. Enclose a card, "Welcome to the world. No one can fill your shoes."

Engraved with Love. Search for a resource for engraving items and have a silver rattle, spoon, frame, or something special engraved with the baby's name and birth date. Personalized items always mean the world to new parents and will become a treasured keepsake.

Here We Grow! Give a photo album, teddy bear, a one-time-use camera, coupons for photo finishing, and signs that help capture baby's week-by-week growth in pictures. Make signs for each week and begin with "Haley is one week old" and end with "Haley is one year old." Add instructions to take the baby's weekly photograph next to the teddy bear and watch baby grow up! This is a fun way to give new parents a memory that will last a lifetime.

Hall of Fame. Be original and give a baby gift of assorted items for baby's milestones. Have a bib personalized with "My first birthday" and include other "hall of fame" moments, like a tooth-fairy pillow or container for baby's first tooth, and a silver spoon for her first spoonful of food. Include a onetime-use camera and a photo album for capturing those pictureperfect moments.

College Fund. Give a monetary gift to boost baby's college fund. Wrap it up with a diploma you create yourself for the new parents giving them a Ph.D. in parenting. Add a note that says, "Congratulations! You have officially entered the world of parenting where every day school is in session."

N

Is for New Home and Hostess Gifts

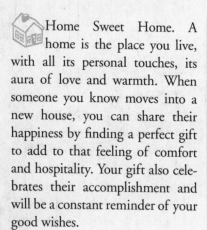Home Sweet Home. A home is the place you live, with all its personal touches, its aura of love and warmth. When someone you know moves into a new house, you can share their happiness by finding a perfect gift to add to that feeling of comfort and hospitality. Your gift also celebrates their accomplishment and will be a constant reminder of your good wishes.

Good manners tell you to bring a gift when you are invited into someone's home. Good sense tells you to make that gift something they'll appreciate, something they can use and enjoy. Hostess gifts needn't be extravagant. After all, you're saying, "Thanks for inviting me." But you also want to make it special and appropriate. Here are some suggestions that will help you accomplish all these goals.

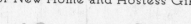New Home Gifts

Home Spotless Home. If friends or family members work or are elderly, give a gift certificate to a reliable cleaning service which can clean their floors, rugs, windows, and bathrooms, leaving the house spotless. Arrange this "clean scene" gift ahead of time and have dinner on the table or in the refrigerator waiting for the new homeowners.

Housewarming. If the new house has a fireplace, bring an armload of wood, some kindling, and a box of fireplace matches. Tell them, "I wanted to give you a REAL housewarming." For a whimsical touch, include a bag of marshmallows for roasting.

Throw in the Sponge. If this is their first home, chances are they could use cleaning supplies. Buy a bucket and fill it with assorted cleaners for the floors, windows, bathrooms, rugs, and appliances.

Throw in some sponges, cleaning supplies, a mop and broom.

Door-to-Door. Show up at the new homeowners' front door with a welcome-home doormat. Choose a style that reflects their taste. Or, consider a personalized doorknocker or assorted, colorful address labels for door-to-door deliveries.

Just the Basics. If they've moved in from out of town, help stock the kitchen with basics. A "first aid" kit of milk, orange juice, butter, bread, cereal, coffee, tea, and sugar. Include local coupons and information about favorite places to shop and other resources in the area.

Photo Finish. Stop by the house and take a photo of it. Have it enlarged and framed. Then, write your well wishes on the back of the frame along with the date and your wisdom for a happy life in the new dwelling. Add a note that says, "Your new home is picture-perfect."

A Touch of Color. If they're moving in during the warm summer months, bring a potted plant that can thrive outdoors in your climate, such as a bright red geranium, a pot of impatiens, or a hanging basket if they have the right spot for it. Add a note that says, "A warm-weather welcome to your new home."

Warm Wishes. Bring a warm dinner while they're settling in, perhaps a casserole or roasted chicken with vegetables, a salad, and cold soft drinks. Include plastic plates and utensils for easy cleanup. Add a card, "Warm wishes for a happy life in your new home. Dinner's on us."

Be My Guest. Think of items that the homeowners will enjoy while entertaining guests. Select guest towels, pretty hand towels, or cocktail napkins and have them monogrammed with their initials. Or, how about a set of placemats and napkins that matches their china?

A Timely Gift. Give a clock chosen to fit the style of their furniture and décor. Add a note that says, "It's about time you settled down. Welcome to your new home."

Moving on Up. Select a scrapbook and insert a photo of the house as it is today presented on the first page. Add a one-time-use camera to memorialize their move and first month in their new home. Write on the front or have a plaque engraved that says, "Home Sweet Home," and the date and year they moved in.

Fixer-Upper. If they're moving into a real fixer-upper, help the process along. Give a toolbox stocked with basics: a hammer, pliers, screwdrivers, a tape measure, nails, and screws. Add a map or gift card with instructions to the nearest hardware or do-it-yourself store. Say, "Hope these hit home with you." If they're new to the homeowner game, give them a book on simple home repairs and upkeep.

Taking the Plunge-r. Choose things most people probably wouldn't think of for gifts, but items that, when you need them, are worth their weight in gold. Buy a plunger, a drain snake, a bottle of drain unclogger, and a tube of tub caulk. Add a note, "Glad you took the plunge. Here are some of life's little necessities."

Don't Forget. Have message pads personalized with their new address and phone number. Add assorted pens and pencils tied with ribbon to keep by the phone.

On a Roll. One of the most traditional of all housewarming gifts is a loaf of freshly baked bread. Include with yours a jar of honey and a pretty cutting board for bread. Say, "Here's some dough for a rainy day!" Or, fill a pretty picnic basket with freshly baked rolls, breads, and muffins and include a note that says, "You're on a roll! Congratulations on your new home."

Pick a Pineapple. In Colonial America, the pineapple was the ultimate symbol of hospitality. Give a pineapple to show yours. Pick a finial if they have a newel post or a topper for the mailbox. Or find an ice bucket or cookie jar shaped like a pineapple.

Feathered Friends. Help your friends settle into their new home with a new house for winged visitors. Choose a pretty birdhouse or bird feeder and offer it with a stock of birdseed. Add a note that says, "May the Bluebird of Happiness land at your door."

Easy Cooking. Choose microwave-to oven-safe cookware or bowls.

Bring over a casserole and heap it with fresh fruit. Include a note that says, "Refills are available on demand."

Gadgets Galore. Consider gifts that are really indulgent like small-sized televisions for kitchen or bathroom countertops, high-tech smoothie makers, shower radios, and compact DVD players. There's an ideal gadget for every room in the house and with a little research you'll score big.

A Spoon Full of Happiness. Give a set of mother-of-pearl-handled spoons, a set of iced teaspoons for entertaining, or a gorgeous serving spoon. Add a note that says, "Many spoons full of happiness in your new home."

Hostess Gifts

Cheese to Please. Purchase a pretty wooden cheeseboard, add two or three wedges of interesting cheeses, and a cheese knife. For good friends with a sense of humor, add a note that says, "A pretty cheesy gift for pretty fabulous friends."

The Coast Is Clear. A set of coasters is always a welcome gift, to save the finish on cherished furniture. Choose durable ones that match their décor, and add a note, "Ring around the glass was a pain in the past. With coasters like these, rings will clean up with ease."

Cordially Yours. Bring a favorite hostess a set of handblown cordial stems or match her crystal pattern, and choose a bottle of peach schnapps for a peachy-keen hostess.

Emergency Chocolates. Everyone has a craving occasionally. Purchase your hostess a box of divine truffles in a pretty tin that the hostess can pass around after dinner or hoard for later. Add a note that says, "Nobody knows the truffles I've seen."

Ready-to-Go Recipes. If your host and hostess pride themselves on their cooking, give them personalized recipe cards so that they can share their culinary creations with friends.

At Her Service. Look for an interesting serving piece in antique silver, perhaps a pickle fork or sugar shell, to enhance her dinner table. Add a note that says, "When it comes to friends, you're a sterling example!"

Music in the Night. Offer a selection of their favorite music with a

CD or two. The accompanying card might say, "An invitation from [their surname] was music to our ears."

Party On. For a large gathering, bring along a one-time-use camera. Discreetly take photos of the party, and mount them in a "brag book" to give the hosts later. Include a note that says, "Party on! It was a picture-perfect party."

Container Mania. If you've been asked to provide an item for the party, bring it in a server that is your gift. Perhaps, a silver-wire breadbasket for rolls, or a serving platter for roasted vegetables. Add a note that says, "I couldn't contain my appreciation. Please enjoy this [item's name] with appreciation from me."

How "Chiming." Select a wind chime. Find one that reflects your hostess's personality. Add a note that tells her how "chiming" she is!

A Grate-ful Gift. If your hosts love Italian food, bring them a wedge of cheese and a cheese grater. Tell them, "We're grate-ful to be your friends."

Sticking Together. A pair of candlesticks is a beautiful gift when they reflect someone's taste and style. From antique to modern, be sure to find out the preferred style and include an assortment of candlesticks that match. Add a note that says, "Friends like us will always 'stick' together."

A First-Hand Gift. Give an indulgent hand cream for hands that do too much or give a manicure at her favorite salon. Wrap up your gift with rubber gloves and a note that says, "Dinner was a handful, and here's a big hand from your fans!"

Kids in Focus. If you are going to someone's home for dinner or to visit and they have kids, bring your gift for the children. Select something age-appropriate the kids will instantly enjoy and a toy their parents will appreciate. Consider a bag of "boredom busters," a videotape or DVD they were hoping for, or a jewelry-making kit for girls, or a hand-held video game for boys.

A Return Visit. Frame a photograph that you took on a previous visit to their home with flowers in bloom in their garden, or give an adorable photograph of their children or pets. Enlarge it and place it in a beautiful frame that matches their décor.

Is for Office Gifts

It seems like every time you turn around, there's an occasion for giftgiving at the office. And why not? You probably spend more hours with your work colleagues than with your family. In a way, they are a second family, with whom you're likely to celebrate holidays, birthdays, weddings, births, promotions, and sad occasions, too. Coworkers, bosses, and clients are all people you'll want to remember on special occasions, holidays, or just to say, "Hi!"

Office etiquette is important to consider when giftgiving, and you never want to outdo other coworkers or put people on the spot. Group gifts where you pool your resources and contributions are always meaningful ideas but be sure to abide if there is a no-gift policy at your company. Also, be aware that gifts that are too personal are not appropriate in an office setting. It's always a good idea to check out what other employees have done in the past,

but don't be afraid to start some new gift-giving traditions, like donating a toy to a good cause, or as a group, adopting a family in need through a homeless shelter. There are multiple opportunities featured in this book for giving gifts of kindness or giving ones that do not cost a thing, so consider your many options.

Coworkers

For a Sweet Coworker! It's a very popular coworker who keeps a bowl or jar of candy on his desk for all to share. If you work with someone like that, make a contribution occasionally. Or, be the one to bring a handsome jar and refill it monthly by mail whenever you visit another office. Include a note or sticker on the jar that says, "To the sweet smell of your success. Thank you! The Spizman Agency."

Budding Opportunities. Bring a coworker a desk enhancer, such as a pretty flower in a vase after a particularly trying day or week. Add a note, "Thanks for keeping your "petal" to the metal. Your help was incredible."

Bear with Me. If you're in the middle of a marathon of hard work and late hours, place a stuffed or ceramic bear on a coworker's desk with a card, "Your hard work is making this project bearable."

Relaxation Balls. The Chinese certainly knew what they were doing when they invented relaxation balls. They're metal balls with a soft chime inside and can be found at many gift or novelty stores. You hold them in one hand and let them rotate, clicking gently together and chiming. The sound is mesmerizing, and the physical sensation very relaxing. A perfect gift for anyone juggling too many balls in the air.

A Star Performer. When someone's been singled out for outstanding performance, reinforce the honor with a star. From star paperweights to jewelry with a star on it, add a note that says, "Congratulations on your stellar performance."

Calling Cards. You've just promoted him, and now he has his own business cards. Order him a card case and have it engraved with his initials. Present it with his first order of cards. Tell him his promotion and success was "in the cards."

Lost Your Marbles? Some days, it feels like you're losing your marbles. If this is happening in your business, present employees with small bags of colored marbles and tell them to hang in there.

On the Fast Track. When a colleague receives a promotion, give him a gift certificate to a sporting-goods store for a new pair of running shoes to celebrate his move up in the company. Your note might read, "Congratulations! Now you're on the fast track."

The Weight of the World. Bosses take note! For an employee who has the weight of the world on his or her shoulders, give her the day of her choice off for some R&R. Few gifts can outdo a paid day off when you really need one.

Initial Impressions. A great gift for any new employee is a handsome leather portfolio embellished with his initials. Add a note that says, "Welcome on board.

Your 'initial' impression was outstanding!"

Happy Days. Welcome back a coworker who's been out sick with a flower and a "We really missed you" banner on her computer screen.

Under the Weather? If a coworker has been ill or having personal problems, buy her a folding umbrella, and add the words, "We're sorry you're under the weather. Count on us if we can ever help!"

On the Ball. Have an employee who is on the ball? Tell her so with tickets for her entire family to a favorite sporting event, or tickets for two to a cause-related charity ball or community event she'd love to attend. Add a note that says, "To an employee who is really on the ball. . . . Have a ball on us!"

Secret Santas. A common holiday tradition in many offices is "Secret Santas." When it's your turn and you have to figure out how to spend the traditional amount of $5 or under, choose his favorite candy bar wrapped up with ribbons and a note that says, "Bar

none, you're the nicest coworker on earth." Or, how about a gift card with $5 applied to a local book, coffee, or DVD rental store in the area she frequents? Add a note that says, "Play your gift 'card' right, and you'll know who I am soon!"

Just Name It. Computers are wonderful things. The right program, a sheet of blank labels, and *presto,* you've got a clever, thoughtful gift. If a coworker is a baker, make her labels for her home-baked goodies. If he's a letter-writer, make him personalized return-address labels. At holiday time, give personalized gift tags for her entire family.

Jotter in a Jiffy. Take note! A really useful gift is a small-sized leather holder that comes with refillable paper called "a jotter." Choose a jotter that can be monogrammed and add a clip-on pen for a useful gift. Also, have the paper personalized as a guaranteed indulgent gift, ideal for the coworker or boss who has everything.

Gifts for the Boss

A "Tee-riffic" Boss. It can be hard giving the boss a gift. But if you know his or her passion, it's much easier. For example, if he's a golfer, give him a mug full of golf tees with a note, "You're really a tee-riffic person to work for!" Or for a tea-loving boss, present her with a selection of teas in a pretty mug. Put them in a gift bag with the note, "You're a tea-riffic boss," or, "As bosses go, you suit us to a tea!"

The Office Pool. Bosses love the affection a gift denotes, but they don't want employees spending lots of money. So how about pooling $5 from each employee and finding one smashing gift instead of a dozen trinkets? A personalized portfolio or attaché case, an updated version of his favorite gadget, that state-of-the-art putter he's been eyeing, or a family portrait with an updated picture for his desk and at home.

Child's Play. She's busy, so are you. If you both have kids, think of her when you're thinking of your kids. Standing in line at 5 A.M. for the latest video game? Pick up an extra for the boss to give her kids. Found a secret stash of the newest baby doll at the local discount store? Get one for her child, too. Or, give a gift amount to a DVD rental store

with a note that says, "Family time is prime time. Enjoy this gift with your entire crew."

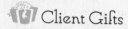 Client Gifts

Shower Your Clients. During the holidays give your clients a lightweight, very small folding umbrella that's purse- or briefcase-sized, or even the other extreme and select a golf umbrella for golfers. Either way, include a note that says, "Showering you with Holiday Wishes."

'Tis the Season. Instead of a single large gift, give clients a fruit or candy basket quarterly, so they'll be reminded of your appreciation throughout the year. Tell them, "'Tis always the season to thank you for your business." Take note if they are health-food lovers and give salt-free nuts and seasonal fruits. Or, start a new tradition and send your gift the week before Thanksgiving to express your thanks ahead of the holiday rush.

Smart Cookies. If you want to compliment your clients for being such "smart cookies," send delicious cookies to their office. Add a note that says, "To the smartest cookies on earth." When selecting cookies, you might search for their preferences, or select ones that come with each cookie individually packaged and which have a longer shelf life. These are ideal for clients who travel or are on the go, so be thoughtful and explore your options when sending anything edible.

Family Affair. Plan ahead for holiday gifts. Buy a block of tickets to a family-oriented circus, ice show, concert, or theater production. Send tickets to clients for themselves and their families, with an invitation to a pre- or post-production lunch or dinner with you and your family.

Ticket for Success. If your company has a box at a sports arena or stadium, offer a pair of tickets to clients. Add a note that says, "Here's a gift of a pair of seats, To one of life's enduring treats. An evening we can't wait to share. We'll confirm the details and see you there."

It's Been a Great Year. Send a huge jar of jellybeans or a basket filled with assorted flavors and small packages for everyone to share, with the sentiment, "It's 'bean' a really great year. Thank you for your business."

Booming and Blooming. If your business is booming, send a colorful plant in bloom to a client and add a note that says, "Thanks for planting your business with us!" Or, "We're in full 'boom' thanks to you!"

P

Is for Party Gifts

A party can be one of the best gifts you could give. Not only does it express your personal sense of devotion, it gives the recipient a chance to mingle with friends and family members, to be the center of attention, and to be recognized in front of those he or she cares about.

What makes a perfect party? Organization, knowing your guests' likes and dislikes, and making everyone who attends feel special and appreciated. Parties needn't be elaborate or expensive to be successful. Just use your imagination, plan carefully, and then enjoy the moment. (Or, at the very least, capture it by taking lots of photographs.)

Keep the food and activities appropriate to the occasion. Remember, there's never too much food or too many choices at a party. With children's parties, match their age and interests to the activity and keep it short and focused. Parties for adults are best served by putting a great mix of people together. Unless it's a reunion or a gathering of your best buds, combine a variety of elements. Add a special twist and purpose to your party. Can't cook? Have a dessert party with a wine tasting and desserts from bakeries in your area, and let everyone vote on their favorite. Add a tarot-card reader and you're destined for a good time. And serve it with pizzazz. Try a mashed-potato bar using martini glasses with lots of toppings or an omelet party (with egg whites available) for healthy eaters.

The secret to a great party, no matter the age of your guests, is always food, creativity, and fun, fun, fun. Pack it in!

Party Tips

Party Animals. Most toddlers have a beloved stuffed animal. Invite kids to bring their favorite stuffed animal to an animal party where they'll also get stuffed! Serve peanut butter sandwiches and instruct the kids on how to transform them with animal-shaped cookie cutters. Have a birthday cake that looks like your child's favorite stuffed friend. Include interactive entertainment like pony rides, a petting zoo, an animal puppet show, or a magician with what else? A stuffed rabbit! Favors could be anything animal-related. Fill a dress-up box with accessories for their stuffed animals with party hats, bracelets, necklaces, and more. Take a photo of each child and their stuffed animal with the birthday boy or girl, and send a copy as a thank-you note and keepsake.

Have a Ball. Children's parties are most successful when there are activities from start to finish. Choose bowling, skating, and gymnastics to keep them busy. For your favorite guests, have a basketball party. Rent out a local gym for an afternoon. Invite teenagers to act as coaches and referees. As guests arrive, divide them into teams by putting a number on each child's hand (Team 1, 2, etc.). Play short quarters: four-to-five minutes, being sure everyone gets a chance to play. Party favors are either small-size basketballs or T-shirts printed with the birthday child's name and the date: "I played basketball with [child's name] at his 8th Birthday Party."

Pop-Star Party. Invite kids to dress up as their favorite pop-star idol. Serve anything that has the word *pop* in it from *pop*sicles, *pop*corn, *pop* tarts to lots of soda *pop*. Invite a hip-hop dancing instructor and give your want-to-be stars a lesson or two. Take photographs of your pop stars with the birthday girl and distribute autographed copies.

Theme Supreme. Theme parties reign supreme. For example, throw a Willy Wonka party. Guests can decorate bags with markers and stickers and then have a candy hunt by sprinkling loads of wrapped candy in the backyard. Or, how about a breakfast party where the guests top-off frosted doughnuts and pancakes with chocolate chips, blueberries, strawberries, and sprinkles? Be creative and whatever theme you choose, be it a breakfast bash or a spend-the-night party, carry it out from start to finish.

Art-Rageous Party. Plan an art party for kids by matching age-appropriate art activities and interests. From making magic wands to pirate hats, tiaras, capes, and tutus, with the right preparation, your party will be a huge success.

An art party can be as simple as stringing noodle necklaces to painting pottery at a pottery store. One clever party was a treasure hunt where the kids searched for all types of stickers and odds and ends, and then decorated a large-paper grocery bag that was transformed into a costume. The parents had cut out arms and a hole for the child's head, and the kids wore their wild and wacky costumes while parading around the backyard.

What's Cooking? Even the tiniest tots love to get involved in the kitchen. With a minimum of help, they can create wonderful snack treats to gobble up at a party and enjoy themselves. Make small round pizzas or use frozen pizzas and let the kids creatively decorate them with toppings. While the items are cooking, entertain the kids with party games you create yourself, like pin the candles on the birthday cake. Or, have lots of candy toppings and icing for instant cup cake decorating for dessert. Use popsicle sticks instead of knifes for a sweet creation on ready-made cakes. Sandwich buffets also are fun and easy to prepare, turning peanut butter sandwiches into funky sandwiches with creative cookie cutters.

Teen Scene. Make sure teen parties reflect their current interests. Host a makeover for a group of teenage girls, with makeup samples as favors. For boys, how about a lesson on basic auto mechanics at the local garage? A mixed group? Music, dancing, and pizza. Or a session of rock climbing or even a scavenger hunt. A Sweet Sixteen party? Check out a spend-the-night party at a swanky hotel with an indoor swimming pool and a chaperone in the room next door—a must!

Halloween Happening. Everyone loves Halloween so have a party that celebrates a junk-food fest. Ask guests to wear costumes all in the same color or from the same era. Transform pizzas into pumpkin faces by having guests decorate cheese pizzas with sliced red peppers, mushrooms, and olives. Make guests a "Boo-quet" of lollipops as a take-home favor by inserting the lollipops into Styrofoam bouquet holders.

Valentine Party. Throw an old-fashioned ice cream social at home or at an ice cream parlor. Decorate the table with candy hearts, pink valentines, and the biggest ice cream sundaes under the sun. Ask guests to wear red and be "red-y" for a good time!

Limo to Go. Arrange ahead of time to surprise your birthday girl or boy by having a limo pick him or her up at school with several preinvited friends. They've got two hours to cruise around town, impressing everyone they know. Stop off and pick up a pizza on the way. Have goody bags and snacks on board for a birthday surprise that will always be remembered. At the end, drop them off at your house for cake and ice cream.

Mommy and Me. Tea parties are a uniquely feminine pursuit for little girls through great-grandmothers. Have a "Mommy and Me" party where you prepare the refreshments together and invite other mommies and daughters to join you. Or splurge on "High Tea" at a local restaurant or hotel, inviting grandmas, aunts, and other special women to join you.

Family Fun-Day. Have a "Sunday Sundae" party. Ask each family to bring a favorite topping. Provide the ice cream, bowls, spoons, and whipped cream. Stand back and watch the fun mount up!

Have a Back to School Bar-B-Que. Celebrate the end of summer with a family get-together before school starts. Play family-oriented games like sack races, egg-in-the-spoon race, water races, and end with a barbecue and indulgent desserts.

Blue Jean Bar/Bat Mitzvah. Many Bar and Bat Mitzvah parties top off the weekend with a festive celebration. From a black-tie bash to a blue jean Bar or Bat Mitzvah, consider creating a party theme around what everyone should wear. From a black-and-white affair to a cruise-wear evening aboard the S. S. Ali, there are many colorful ways to add a festive touch. Create meaningful centerpieces with baskets of food that can be later donated to the hungry or a homeless shelter or plants that could be planted in honor of your guests at a senior citizens' home.

Sweet Sixteen. Throw your sweet sixteen-year-old an indulgent dessert party with a decadent dessert bar. Set the table with parfait glasses filled with candy and add a straw to top it off as the perfect party favor. Pour on the junk food and serve ice cream sundaes for the sweetest sixteen-year-old you know. Or, how about High Tea with fancy finger sandwiches and pickup sweets.

Ladies That Lunch. Planning a birthday luncheon? Make it memorable. Think pink and throw a totally pink party for ladies who lunch. Tell guests to wear pink and decorate everything with a pink theme. Or, have an advice luncheon. Include blank cards in the invitations and ask guests to bring their best tip for shopping or even staying young. Fill a pretty box with the tips and present it to the guest of honor.

Grown-Ups Are Kids Too! Adult parties don't have to be stiff, formal affairs. Make yours fun. Give a '50s sock hop, a '60s hippie party. Or a "Come as You Were" party wearing a blast from the past, with guests asked to come dressed as they were at a certain age or in a certain year.

Over the Hill. Make that aging milestone less depressing with an "Over the Hill Party," appropriate for any "big" birthday from forty on. Ask guests to dress in black and bring humorous gifts... some gingko biloba for memory loss, perhaps?

Grown-up Pursuits. Theme parties are great for grown-ups. Give a "Novel Party" and ask each guest to bring a book they've enjoyed, wrapped in plain paper, for a blind exchange. Have a cookie exchange at the holidays, complete with printed recipes to share. Guests can make ten copies, so that everyone can take a cookie-recipe collection home. Throw a "Snack Attack Super Bowl Party" and request that guests bring a favorite munchie. Assign some sweet, some salty. Or, how about a "Popcorn Party" and watch an episode of a popular TV show? Cook together, making an entire meal to be shared later. Taste wines and chocolates. Make chocolates. Hire a dance instructor or a chef. Fun is the focus!

Invitations

Sensational Certificate. Print invitations to look like a certificate or a diploma. "This hereby certifies that so-and-so is invited...." This works particularly well for a graduation party. Roll the certificate inside a mailing tube for a surprise delivery.

Special Delivery. For a REALLY special occasion have invitations marked "hand-delivered" on the envelope and presented by a tuxedo-clad man in a limousine, or a cowboy on horseback, or a motorcycle mama. Anything goes!

Picture a Party. Send a mirror with the invitation tied or stuck to it. The message would read, "Picture yourself partying with [host's name] on January 28th!"

Facing Fifty! For a fiftieth birthday, combine a full-faced photograph with an invitation that reads, "Willy's facing fifty."

Paper Caper. Handmade paper, calligraphy, pressed dried flowers behind parchment, glitter paper, metallic inks on shiny paper, ribbons and bows, lace . . . make your invitation reflect your personality.

Oh Boy, It's a Girl. Combine a play on words and be clever. Write "Oh boy, oh boy, oh boy" on the outside and "It's a girl" on the inside of the note. It's a clever birth announcement or invitation to a baby naming.

Words on Paper. Aside from the basics, tell your guests what's happening with a poem.

Carla's turning fifty.
We think that's nifty.

So won't you come
And join the fun.

A word to the wise,
It's a surprise
We're trying to keep,
So not even a peep!

On a High Note. Want a really unique party invitation? Send each invitee a singing telegram, to be delivered at his or her home or place of work. Have the delivery person hand a written invitation as well, of course, printed on yellow paper to look like a traditional telegram. This also works with someone singing the invitation on the telephone and a follow-up version sent in the mail.

We Reserved a Spot! Find a polka-dotted paper for your invitation and add these words: "We've reserved a spot for you at Ali's Sweet Sixteen Surprise Party." Or, "There's a spot in our hearts for Grandma Phyllis—Please help us celebrate!"

Don't Let the Cat Out of the Bag! Giving a surprise party? Tell the guests not to let the cat out of the bag and send your invite in an actual paper bag. Seal it with a colorful cat sticker for a purrrr-fect surprise.

Party Favors, Memory Makers, and Place Cards

Match the Theme. Party favors are what your guests will take home with them, a tangible reminder of the fabulous party you gave. Favors needn't be expensive, just thoughtful and original. Sometimes a visit to the dollar store will spark an idea, like votive candles and flowerpots you can personalize with guests' names and fill with candy. Some party favors lend themselves to personalizing. Consider packets of flower seeds used in the centerpieces or bridal bouquet, candy bars with guests' names printed on a label and used as place cards, treat boxes filled with candy or personalized notepads.

Cookie Cutters. Cookie cutters are a clever party favor to give out at a bridal shower. They can also be used to creatively top off a present at a kitchen shower or as a gift for your favorite baker. Tie a cookie cutter to a notecard that reads: "Doug and Genie were cut out for each other!" Or, give an assortment of cookie cutters with a note that reads: "We were cut out to be friends."

Two-in-One. Your place card can also be a favor to take home. These might include a picture frame with the guest's name written in calligraphy and placed in the frame, tiny flashlights or paperweights with each guest's name on it and the date of the party. Also consider silver-plated miniature baskets with a card inserted, personalized water bottles, or scented candles with guests' names on them.

Time in a Bottle. At a recent wedding we attended, the bride's sister (her maid of honor) collected words of wisdom for the bride and groom from all the guests throughout the wedding weekend. She filled a beautiful box with everyone's best advice and gave instructions to the happy couple to open and read on their first wedding anniversary. This gift was sealed with a kiss, her words of wisdom, and will be a special gift they will look forward to opening. She also included a bottle of champagne from the wedding weekend to toast the occasion.

Poetic Place Card. Consider small picture frames for place cards. Write your guests' names on a card in the frame, or write individual, personalized poems for each guest for a gift they're sure to cherish. The poems can reflect how much you adore the guest or something special about them. For example

Grandma and Grandpa,
we love you so,
Through the years you watched
us grow.
You've loved us from the very start,
You'll forever be inside our hearts.

Our dearest son Justin,
what can we say?
Except having you home is
a joyous day!

Dearest Ali, as daughters go,
You're the world's best a parent
could know.
Being with you puts a smile
on our face.
No one could ever take your place.

Is for Quotable-Quotes

The right words at the right time can really be a challenge, and sometimes you're simply at a loss for what to say. That's the best time to let someone else do the talking. Here's a selection of heartfelt and inspiring quotes that have endured time and might just fill the bill, or help you find the words of your own that you're looking for.

Quotations are the perfect choice for sprucing up a thank-you note, toast, speech, or a way to give the ultimate compliment or to commemorate an occasion. The following quotes will help you sum up your thoughts and give you a jump-start for expressing your feelings.

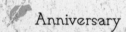
Anniversary

Let us be grateful to people who make us happy, they are the charming gardeners who make our souls blossom.
—*Marcel Proust*

Happiness makes up in height for what it lacks in length.
—*Robert Frost*

Birthday

Old age is not so bad when you consider the alternative.
—*Maurice Chevalier*

You know you are getting old when the candles cost more than the cake.
—*Bob Hope*

Just say, I'm not 50, I'm 18 with 32 years experience.
—*Unknown*

Wrinkles should merely indicate where smiles have been.
—*Mark Twain*

Encouragement

Remember, no one can make you feel inferior without your consent.
—*Eleanor Roosevelt*

We can do anything we want to if we stick to it long enough.
—*Helen Keller*

Courage is grace under pressure.
—*Ernest Hemingway*

Faith

Faith is a passionate intuition.
—*William Wordsworth*

Family

Where we love is home—home that our feet may leave, but not our hearts.
—*Oliver Wendell Holmes, Sr.*

Forgiveness

I can forgive, but I cannot forget, is only another way of saying, I will not forgive. Forgiveness ought to be like a cancelled note—torn in two, and burned up, so that it never can be shown against one.
—*Henry Ward Beecher*

Forgiveness is the fragrance the violet sheds on the heel that has crushed it.
—*Mark Twain*

Friendship

In everyone's life, at some time, our inner fire goes out. It is then burst into flame by an encounter with another human being. We should all be thankful for those people who rekindle the inner spirit.
—*Albert Schweitzer*

A friend is a gift you give yourself.
—*Robert Louis Stevenson*

There are three great friends: an old wife, an old dog, and ready money.
—*Benjamin Franklin*

The most I can do for my friend is simply be his friend.
—*Henry David Thoreau*

The language of friendship is not words but meanings.
—*Henry David Thoreau*

Nothing but heaven itself is better than a friend who is really a friend.
—*Plautus*

He who has a thousand friends has not a friend to spare, and he who has one enemy will meet him everywhere.
—*Ralph Waldo Emerson*

It is not so much our friends' help that helps us, as the confidence of their help.
—*Epicurus*

But friendship is precious, not only in the shade, but in the sunshine of life, and thanks to a benevolent arrangement the greater part of life is sunshine.
—*Thomas Jefferson*

The ornament of a house is the friends who frequent it.
—*Ralph Waldo Emerson*

It is one of the blessings of old friends that you can afford to be stupid with them.
—*Ralph Waldo Emerson*

Ah, how good it feels! The hand of an old friend.
—*Henry Wadsworth Longfellow*

A man's growth is seen in the successive choirs of his friends.
—*Ralph Waldo Emerson*

Friendship is a single soul dwelling in two bodies.
—*Aristotle*

I have friends in overalls whose friendship I would not swap for the favor of the kings of the world.
—*Thomas A. Edison*

 Grief

It's so curious: one can resist tears and "behave" very well in the hardest hours of grief. But then someone makes you a friendly sign behind a window, or one notices that a flower that was in bud only yesterday has suddenly blossomed, or a letter slips from a drawer . . . and everything collapses.
—*Colette*

While grief is fresh, every attempt to divert only irritates. You must wait till it be digested, and then amusement will dissipate the remains of it.
—*Samuel Johnson*

If you're going through hell, keep going.
—*Winston Churchill*

If you suppress grief too much, it can well redouble.
—*Moliere*

She was no longer wrestling with the grief, but could sit down with it as a lasting companion and make it a sharer in her thoughts.
—*George Eliot*

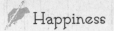 Happiness

The best way to cheer yourself is to try to cheer somebody else up.
—*Mark Twain*

Pleasure is spread through the earth
In stray gifts to be claimed by whoever shall find.
—*William Wordsworth*

Happiness is like a butterfly which, when pursued, is always beyond our grasp, but, if you will sit down quietly, may alight upon you.
—*Nathaniel Hawthorne*

He is rich or poor according to what he is, not according to what he has.
—*Henry Ward Beecher*

My crown is called content, a crown that seldom kings enjoy.
—*William Shakespeare*

Be happy. It's one way of being wise.
—*Colette*

Pleasure is very seldom found where it is sought. Our brightest blazes are commonly kindled by unexpected sparks.
—*Samuel Johnson*

Happiness is when what you think, what you say, and what you do are in harmony.
—*Mahatma Gandhi*

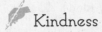 Kindness

Those who bring sunshine to the lives of others cannot keep it from themselves.
—*James M. Barrie*

The manner of giving is worth more than the gift.
—*seventeenth-century playwright Corneille*

I always prefer to believe the best of everybody, it saves so much trouble.
—*Rudyard Kipling*

No person was ever honored for what he received. Honor has been the reward for what he gave.
—*Calvin Coolidge.*

Kindness is the language which the deaf can hear and the blind can see.
—*Mark Twain*

Kindness gives birth to kindness.
—*Sophocles*

It is more blessed to give than to receive.
—*Acts 20:35*

Wherever there is a human being, there is an opportunity for a kindness.
—*Seneca*

Always be a little kinder than necessary.
—*James M. Barrie*

Kindness is in our power, even when fondness is not.
—*Samuel Johnson*

The best portion of a good man's life—his little, nameless, unremembered acts of kindness and love.
—*William Wordsworth*

You cannot do a kindness too soon, for you never know how soon it will be too late.
—*Ralph Waldo Emerson*

By swallowing evil words unsaid, no one has ever harmed his stomach.
—*Winston Churchill*

One man cannot hold another man down in the ditch without remaining down in the ditch with him.
—*Booker T. Washington*

How far that little candle throws his beams!
So shines a good deed in a weary world.
—*William Shakespeare*

I expect to pass through life but once. If therefore, there be any kindness I can show, or any good thing I can do to any fellow being, let me do it now, and not defer or neglect it, as I shall not pass this way again.
—*William Penn*

The greatest good you can do for another is not just to share your riches but to reveal to him his own.
—*Benjamin Disraeli*

 Life

The purpose of life is a life of purpose.
—*Robert Byrne*

Just living is not enough. One must have sunshine, freedom, and a little flower.
—*Hans Christian Anderson*

An aim in life is the only fortune worth finding. And it is not to be found in foreign lands, but in the heart itself.
—*Robert Louis Stevenson*

You only live once, but if you do it right, once is enough.
—*Mae West*

To live is so startling it leaves little time for anything else.
—*Emily Dickinson*

The price of anything is the amount of life you exchange for it.
—Henry David Thoreau

In three words I can sum up everything I've learned about life. It goes on.
—Robert Frost

A long life may not be good enough, but a good life is long enough.
—Benjamin Franklin

Love and Marriage

Doubt that the stars are fire, doubt that the sun doth move, doubt truth to be a liar, but never doubt I love.
—William Shakespeare

Love adds a precious seeing to the eye.
—William Shakespeare

Love looks not with the eyes, but with the mind,
And therefore is winged Cupid painted blind.
—William Shakespeare, A
  Midsummer-Night's
  Dream, 1595

If you judge people, you have no time to love them.
—Mother Teresa

I love you not only for what you are, but for what I am when I am with you. I love you not only for what you have made of yourself, but for what you are making of me. I love you for the part of me that you bring out.
—Elizabeth Barrett Browning

'Tis better to have loved and lost than never to have loved at all.
—Alfred, Lord Tennyson

Love is an irresistible desire to be irresistibly desired.
—Robert Frost

A loving heart is the truest wisdom.
—Charles Dickens

A man is not where he lives, but where he loves.
—Latin proverb

At the touch of love, everyone becomes a poet.
—Plato

The supreme happiness of life is the conviction that we are loved— loved for ourselves, or rather, loved in spite of ourselves.
—Victor Hugo

Love is a canvas furnished by Nature and embroidered by imagination.
—Voltaire

Making a Difference

I have found the paradox that if I love until it hurts, then there is no hurt, but only more love.
—*Mother Teresa*

Act as if what you do makes a difference. It does.
—*William James*

Nobody made a greater mistake than he who did nothing because he could only do a little.
—*Edmund Burke*

If you can't feed a hundred people, then feed just one.
—*Mother Teresa*

Wherever a man turns he can find someone who needs him.
—*Albert Schweitzer*

I am of the opinion that my life belongs to the whole community and as long as I live, it is my privilege to do for it whatever I can. I want to be thoroughly used up when I die, for the harder I work the more I live.
—*George Bernard Shaw*

The only gift is a portion of thyself.
—*Ralph Waldo Emerson*

Not only must we be good, but we must also be good for something.
—*Henry David Thoreau*

Every individual has a place to fill in the world and is important in some respect whether he chooses to be so or not.
—*Nathaniel Hawthorne*

You must be the change you wish to see in the world.
—*Mahatma Gandhi*

Let no one ever come to you without leaving better and happier.
—*Mother Teresa*

Have courage for the great sorrows of life and patience for the small ones; and when you have laboriously accomplished your daily task, go to sleep in peace.
—*Victor Hugo*

R

Is for Right-from-the-Heart Gifts

What better gift than one that is straight from the heart? Heartfelt gifts endure time and remind someone how much they are thought of and cherished. Gifts from the heart also include your presence. Sometimes a new sweater or object just doesn't capture your feelings or express the depth of feeling you want to convey with a gift. For those occasions, consider giving a gift from your heart, for the good of the world and the good of others.

Charitable or helpful gifts can range from cash, donations, merchandise, or the contribution of your time and talents to another's life. Gifts from the heart can be known to the receiver or often can remain anonymous. Tailor your gift to the occasion, need, or desires of the person you are trying to help or honor. Gifts from the heart enter the heart. What could be better?

A Heartfelt Gift. One of the most endearing things you can do is to show your altruism and honor a friend by making a charitable contribution. Just be sure to choose a charity that matches your friend's beliefs and interests. Your donation need not just be money; you can donate time, food, and other material things as well. Cook for a homeless shelter or buy prayer books for a church in someone else's honor. Send a card or note to let him know. Examples follow:

"You're a tree-mendous friend! That's why I've planted a tree in your honor."

"To one of the warmest people I know: Winter jackets have been given to the shelter in your name."

"Instead of going out to dinner, I cooked for the homeless shelter last night in honor of your contributions to the community."

"Read all about it! Your name is on the bookplate of six new books at our local hospital's library."

Food for Thought. Most communities have a soup kitchen or community food bank. Want to teach a young person the value of giving from the heart? Have him accompany you to one of these centers and spend an afternoon or evening serving food to those less fortunate. Make it a family tradition and do it as often as possible.

School Days. Before school starts for the year, visit the sales at your local discount store and stock up on school supplies. Fill a book bag with a notebook, paper, pens, a ruler, glue, scissors. Bring these to a homeless shelter before classes start, to be given to children who can't afford to buy supplies for themselves.

Fired Up. Think of your local firemen and policemen and create a day to honor them. Involve your kids or classroom students. Write thank-you notes to each fireman and policeman, and personalize the notes. Bake cakes and bring home-baked goods to say "thank you" to our everyday heroes.

A Jewel of a Gift. Here's a meaningful gift that a New York birthstone jeweler named Keith Saxe did to honor the memory of his beloved aunt. After she passed away, he gave each of her daughters a birthstone necklace to be worn close to their hearts. The mother's birthstone was placed above the daughters', as a symbol of her looking down on each of them. Their birthstone necklaces have been treasured for years and, to this day, are a beloved gift the daughters continue to wear.

Teaching from the Heart. Teach your child about giving from the heart with a gift to one of the many children's charities. When buying your child a book or toy, purchase a duplicate and drop it off at a shelter or children's hospital.

Community Coat Closet. Encourage and help a youngster run a clothing drive among friends and schoolmates, and then go together to deliver the clothes to a school or community center that distributes garments to those who are in need. Make sure the clothes are clean and in wearable condition.

Walk for the Cause. There are many diseases that have inspired walks to raise money to search for cures. Participate in one in honor of a survivor, or sadly, in memory of a victim. Have their likeness printed on a T-shirt. Wear it as you walk, and send the family a photo of you on the walk, with a note telling how much that individual did to inspire you.

Reading for the Blind. Various groups offer books on tape and Braille books for the blind. Consider volunteering your time to help by auditioning to be a reader.

The Grass Is Greener. Everything's greener when you tend to it. Get your garden club to adopt a senior citizens' home as a year-round gardening project. Let the residents know that their lives have inspired your group's love of nurturing life.

Giving Thanks. On Thanksgiving or any day of the year, help your children learn to give thanks by teaching them to share. Each major holiday, drop off toys and books at a children's hospital or day-care center for the underprivileged. As they grow, let your kids earn the money to purchase these gifts.

Pretty Is as Pretty Does. Does anyone in your family travel? Have them collect the small toiletries supplied in hotel rooms. Make bags with these items, and include tissues, Band-Aids, and other necessities to take to a local women's or homeless shelter.

Write from the Heart. Do you love to write? Do you have great penmanship? Visit a senior citizens' home once a week and help residents with their correspondence or recording their life story. Bring a selection of pretty stationery, pens, and stamps along to give anonymously to those who can't get out.

Gimme Shelter. Imagine yourself with no roof over your head, and it's raining. Purchase a supply of umbrellas to keep in your car. When you see someone in the rain without cover, offer an umbrella and give him shelter.

A "Tree-Mendous" Gift. Know someone who has "tree-mendously" impacted your life? Plant a tree in his or her honor at a special location that would be meaningful to him or her. Organizations here and overseas have forests dedicated to the honor of special people or even to the memory of loved ones. You can also do it yourself if you have a green thumb.

Play It Safe. Inspect a loved one's home for safety hazards. Make sure she or he has a carbon-monoxide detector, operating fire alarm, fire extinguisher, nonslip mats in tubs, and a hazard-free environment. What better gift than keeping someone you care about safe?

Sealed with a Kiss. Write a letter to a parent or someone you love describing how he or she has made a significant difference in your life. Be specific and think of all the ways your life has been inspired. You can never write enough of these letters, and they will become a timeless treasure over the years. Or, if you're a grandparent, parent, or special friend, write a letter of wisdom that will impact another's life in an inspiring way. Share lessons you've learned and insights you'd like to pass on.

Forgiveness. If someone has hurt you or you've hurt someone and you wish to repair the relationship, reach out to that person often. If you really care about them, don't give up. Forgiveness and acceptance are gifts only the heart can offer, and often there's work to be done that doesn't meet the eye. From writing letters of kindness to words of apology, your options are many.

S

Is for Special-Day Gifts

Giftgiving is an around-the-year activity thanks to all the special days sprinkled throughout the calendar year. Special days, holidays, and commemorative occasions are things we look forward to. We all have our favorite events to celebrate and often they are meaningful gift-giving opportunities. Special days offer us many opportunities for creating family traditions and to celebrate times of togetherness. These personal, family-oriented times are occasions we all look forward to, and the following ideas will help you add a touch of festivity to the occasion.

Here's a list, month-by-month, of those calendar days with gift-giving suggestions, and some ideas for creating your own "special days."

Please note: Refer to *H* Is for Holidays, *V* Is for Valentine's Day, and other related sections for additional gift ideas for special days.

January

New Year's Day. January 1 starts off the Western calendar year. It's a day for visiting, for making New Year's resolutions, for watching parades and football games. A gift of homemade cookies or a new recipe book for spicing up the year ahead is a fun New Year's gift. Or, offer some humor by giving a cactus to someone who doesn't need to "turn over a new leaf this year."

Eastern Orthodox Christmas. January 6. Celebrating this rite is similar to the more familiar December Christmas date. Gifts to loved ones and friends should express joy, love, and fellowship.

Martin Luther King's Birthday. Observed on the third Monday in January, Martin Luther King Day celebrates the birthday of the great civil-rights leader. In his honor give the gift of a dream fulfilled by donating children's "birthday" gifts to a local Boys or Girls Club on King's birthday. Or, make a contribution of a book about MLK to their center or library. Children could earn and then deliver the gifts as their way of paying homage to a great man's ideals.

February

Groundhog Day. Every February 2, the groundhog ascends from his den. If he sees his shadow, we'll have six more weeks of winter. If he doesn't, our gift is an early spring. Offer a friend a picture in a shadow box in honor of Punxatawney Phil, the world's most famous groundhog and weather animal, with a photograph of you and your favorite shadow or sidekick.

Valentine's Day. The day for lovers. Give your love a dozen roses plus one in a different color for your love to grow on. Add a card that says, "A dozen roses which symbolize my love for you, plus one for us to grow on." Also, call her or him every hour on the hour to register your love. Don't forget a pretty card, full of hearts, lace, ribbons and loving sentiments.

Presidents' Day. Combining the birthdays of Presidents Washington and Lincoln, Presidents' Day is celebrated on the third Monday in February. On this special day do a good deed and promote citizenship. Welcome a new citizen of our country who you know by bringing over a hot dinner or send a book about the president who inspired you most.

Chinese New Year. Different calendar, different dates each year. The celebration calls for festivities and feasts. Surprise a friend with a feast of take-out Chinese food, complete with chopsticks and fortune cookies. "Any day is a happy New Year's Day when I can celebrate it with you."

March

The Luck of the Green. March 17 is St. Patrick's Day, the day of the Irish. Wear green and get kissed, wear orange and get pinched. Give an Irish friend the traditional St. Patrick's Day gift of home-baked soda bread. If you can't bake it, buy it. And wrap it in green paper. Or, give a box of Lucky Charms® to all your friends and let them know it's your lucky day because you are friends.

Spring Is Sprung. The Vernal Equinox, the first day of spring, occurs on March 20, 21, or 22, depending on the year. It's a perfect day for a gift of cheery daffodils, precursors of warm weather ahead and flowery sentiments. "Spring is sprung, the grass is green. You're the prettiest girl, I've ever seen!"

April

April Fool's Day. There's only one way to give a gift for this day—make it a gag gift, a joke. Did you win the lottery (not)? Give a book of jokes, or play a gentle trick, yell "April Fool," and make up for it with gifts fit for your favorite fool.

Secretary's Day. Give your secretary something that will be dazzling on her desk, along with a CD or DVD of her favorite Broadway show. Add a note that says, "Your hard work takes center stage, and your fans applaud you today and every day."

Movable Feasts. Because of different calendars, many spring religious holidays fall on different dates each year. In the Christian faith, Lent begins forty days before Easter, and Good Friday on the Friday before Easter Sunday. In the Jewish faith, Purim and Passover are celebrated during this time period.

Easter. Christianity's most significant holiday is both solemn and celebratory. Easter lilies symbolize the resurrection. The favorite Easter gift for all ages is the traditional Easter basket, filled with chocolate bunnies, dyed eggs, and sweets of all kinds. From dime-store toys to beautiful handblown glass bunnies and other indulgent eggs that are works of art, include them all and add a card that says, "Some-bunny loves you very much!"

Purim. Purim is the feast of lots celebrated by Jewish people, remembering the story of Esther, who saved her people from genocide in Biblical times. Gifts of food, especially three-cornered pastries called *hamantaschen*, are given at this time of year. "I made these myself for you to eat, because our friendship's such a treat."

Passover. Passover, or Pesach, is a Jewish holiday that tells of the escape of the Jewish people from slavery in Egypt. It lasts eight days, during which no leavened food is eaten. If you're invited to a Seder, or holiday feast, bring a bottle of wine that's marked "Kosher for Passover," or a box of candy with the same label. Scour old bookstores and find an old Hagaddah (the book of stories and prayers used at the Seder). Or, select a beautiful Seder plate or wine goblet for Elijah.

Hajj. This holiday commemorates the pilgrimage to Mecca, which is a commandment for religious Muslims to undertake at least once in a life. If you are celebrating with a Muslim family, give a donation to help a child learn.

May

May Day. May 1 is May Day. It is an international celebration of love, life, and rejuvenation. May-poles, floral wreaths, picnics, and songs are May Day traditions. Give your love a photograph of beautiful flowers enlarged and frame it with a note that says, "Every day with you is a special day, here's a beautiful flower that welcomes in May."

Cinco De Mayo. May 5 is the Mexican national holiday cele-brated with festivities, parades, and special traditional foods. Fill a basket with musical instruments, noisemakers the kids can make from paper-towel tubing, plus hot sauces and Mexican specialties.

Mother's Day. One of our most beloved holidays, Mother's Day falls on the second Sunday in May. Honor Mom and Grand-mother with flowers, candy, and perfume; take them out to dinner. Let them know they are the center of your family's universe. See "*M* Is for Mom" for more ways to indulge and make her feel special.

Memorial Day. Originally May 31, Memorial Day is now cele-brated on the last Monday in May. It is a day to remember and honor those who gave their lives in service to their country. Honor them by visiting graves, attending parades, and making donations in their names to veterans' associations.

June

Flag Day. June 14 is the official day to honor the red, white, and blue of the U.S. flag. Make sure your flag is clean, in good repair, and is flying properly. If not, retire it honorably and purchase a new one to display today and every day.

Father's Day. Dad's own special day is the third Sunday in June. Shower him with gifts he wouldn't buy for himself, and let him know how important he is to you, even if you're grown and gone with kids of your own. Don't forget Grandpa either on this important day. Present him with a trophy, engraved, "Anybody can be a father, but it takes a special person to be a dad. Thanks for being the world's best dad!"

Here Comes Summer. Summer officially begins on June 20, 21, or 22. It's also the longest day of the year. Make it a family day with a trip to the beach or pool, if it's warm enough. Give a summer basket of lemonade, sun-block lotion, sunglasses, and a beach towel to a sun-loving friend, a hot mamma, or kid who loves the outdoors.

 July

Independence Day. The Fourth of July. Firecracker Day. Cookouts and fireworks displays. Give a patriotic gift: a biography of John Adams, George Washington, or Thomas Jefferson, or a video of the movie *1776*, which dramatizes the struggle for independence. For a child, put together a plastic jar filled with layers of red, white, and blue jelly beans.

 September

Labor Day. Labor Day, the first Monday in September, is a creation of the labor movement and is dedicated to the social and economic achievements of American workers. It constitutes a yearly national tribute to the contributions workers have made to the strength, prosperity, and well-being of our country. Prepare a lavish picnic and invite your friends and family to a "labor (day) of love."

Grandparents' Day. The first Sunday in September following Labor Day is Grandparents Day. Grandmas and Grandpas appreciate home-made gifts that express a child's love and show how much they are adored. From handwritten poems to works of art, display your affection to perfection, and show your grandparents there is no one grander!

The High Holy Days. The Jewish New Year, (Rosh Hashanah) and the

Day of Atonement (Yom Kippur), fall in September or October. If invited to share one of these holidays, or to break the fast following Yom Kippur, send flowers ahead of time to be used as a table centerpiece or to brighten their home. Or, offer to make a honey cake, which is a tradition for the New Year, and bring it along with a jar of honey and a basket of apples to be cut into slices for dipping in the honey to symbolize a sweet New Year.

Fall for Fall. Autumn officially begins on September 20, 21, or 22. Day and night are of equal length. Celebrate with a basket of crunchy apples or autumn vegetables. Add a note saying, "When I harvested friends, you were my first pick."

October

Columbus Day. October 12 is the traditional birthday celebration for Christopher Columbus, discoverer of America. Give a globe to commemorate this brave explorer or fill a box with foods or spices from around the world. Add a note that says, "If I traveled the whole world though, I couldn't find a better friend than you. Happy Columbus Day."

Halloween. October 31 is the holiday of ghosts, goblins, and things that go bump in the night. It has its origins in old pagan mysteries. But there's nothing mysterious about a carved jack o'lantern with a candle glowing inside or a big bucket of candy waiting to be handed out to trick-or-treaters. Halloween is a gift for everyone to enjoy. If you bought too much candy or the kids bags are overflowing, sort only sealed candy by colors, and layer it in recycled jars in rainbow layers for creative holiday gifts you can drop off at a senior citizens' home or shelter on the next day. "No tricks, just treats." Another fun tradition is to 'Boo' someone. Start a neighborhood tradition and every year have a boo-a-thon and surprise a neighbor with a bag of treats left at the front door. Someone starts it each year and leaves a note for the next person to continue. Once you've been boo'd, tie a ribbon or post the note at your door. The note should say

Someone thinks you're
a treat to know!
Now boo another neighbor—
it's your turn to go!
Once you've been boo'd,
tie a ribbon at your door,
And then go "boo" another

*neighbor—with sweet treats
in store.*

National Boss's Day. Check out this year's date for this October holiday.

Write a letter of appreciation and share with the boss what he or she has taught you. Your words of appreciation and thanks will be appreciated most of all.

November

Election Day. Election Day is the first Tuesday in November. Give a gift to the politician of your choice by casting a vote. Then send a card to someone who has your vote and whom you adore!

Veterans' Day. November 11 is the day we honor our veterans, those men and women who have served in the armed forces to protect and defend us. Give them the gift of your respect, at a parade or national cemetery. Make candy jars for vets at the VA hospital, using red, white, and blue hard candies and adding patriotic stickers. Drop them off with thank-you notes as your way to say, "We appreciate YOU-S-A! Thank you for being there when our country needed you."

Thanksgiving. In the U.S., Thanksgiving is celebrated on the fourth Thursday in November. Start a family tradition and send out Thanksgiving cards instead of holiday cards to express your thanks. Also, check with local shelters and organizations to find a center or family to whom you can donate food items and provide Thanksgiving dinner.

December

Hanukkah. The Festival of Lights falls anywhere from very late November to the end of December. In the Jewish calendar, it is celebrated on the twenty-fifth day of Kislev. Hanukkah means "dedication," and commemorates the victory of the Maccabees. Visit a local synagogue gift shop or Judaica store to find a varied selection of gifts. Start a child or family member on a collection of dreidels and spin your way into their hearts during this holiday that celebrates the miracle of how one day's worth of oil burned for eight days.

Ramadan. Ramadan is the ninth month of the Muslim calendar. It is during this month that Muslims observe the Fast of Ramadan. Lasting for the entire month, Muslims fast during the daylight hours and in the evening eat small meals and visit with friends and family. It is a time of worship and contemplation. A time to strengthen family and community ties. Give moon and star-shaped cookie cutters or Ramadan-decorated paper plates.

Christmas. December 25 is the day Western Christians celebrate Jesus' birth, with gifts galore, holly, mistletoe, carols, and parties. Give a gift with tradition, a porcelain angel or ornament for the Christmas tree, a recording of Christmas carols, a basket of sugarplums wrapped in red and green with a big, bright bow. Or give a gift of good tidings. Take an elderly person a box of Christmas cards, a green pen, and a roll of stamps. Offer to help address his or her cards and mail them.

Kwanzaa. The African American holiday of Kwanzaa lasts from December 26 through January 1. It is a holiday affirming the accomplishments of the African American community, stressing family strength and unity. Bring homemade gifts of food or traditional African craft objects. "May your holiday grow, like your children, from strength to strength."

Your Own Special Days

This Is Your Day. Check out the Chase Calendar of Events at www.chases.com for a marvelous book listing over twelve thousand special days, weeks, months, birthdays, anniversaries, holidays, fairs, and festivals. When there's someone you want to honor, this resource is wonderful. It will help you find the perfect time to say a big thank you to a teacher on National Teachers' Day, or Take Your Daughter to Work Day, or Breast Cancer Awareness, or Canada Day, or Russian Orthodox Easter.

Bar/Bat Mitzvah. A Bar Mitzvah (for a boy) or Bat Mitzvah (for a girl) is a very special day symbolizing adulthood in the life of a Jewish thirteen-year-old, and it requires a great deal of studying and hard work. Consider a meaningful present that commemorates this event, like a mezuzah, a Star of David necklace, silver candlesticks (for a girl), or their very own Hanukkah menorah. Or, when giving a check, add extra to your gift and request that they keep a portion and give the additional amount to a good cause in honor of their special day. For example, you could give

$25, with $18 (the number that stands for *chai*, meaning "life") as your gift, and request that the additional $7 be donated to a charity of their choice. Most Bar and Bat Mitzvahs send an invitation to their special day. Framing it is another way to commemorate the occasion, or purchase a shadowbox or beautiful treasure box and give it with their invitation included and instructions to save their keepsakes. Other favorite gifts for girls include silver jewelry, heart necklaces, or a jewelry box. For boys, consider sports memorabilia, a personalized money clip, or high-tech gadgets. And if in doubt, select a gift card, gift certificate, or a check is always a great choice.

School Days. School days mark important milestones for children. Celebrate the first day of school, the last day, and graduation day with gifts that emphasize learning. For the start of school, give a new book bag or fittings for the locker. For the end of the school year, a book to start summer reading, or a stay-up-late sleepover with friends. For graduation, give a gift that summarizes your pride in the child's accomplishment, perhaps a trip to an amusement park, a gift of money, or a shopping spree.

Recitals. Treat a recital as you would an adult's promotion or new job. A child has worked exceedingly hard to come to this level of mastery. Give a girl a corsage, a new dress. For a boy, a wallet, new suit, or CD. Take plenty of photos and make a "brag book" and be sure the child sees your pride in it and in her or him. "I always knew you could dance (or sing, or act, or play an instrument). Now the world knows it, too!"

Religious Celebrations. There are many other religious occasions ranging from baptisms, communions, to confirmations. Engraved or personalized gifts that commemorate the date and event are appreciated, as well as necklaces with religious charms or symbols, and personalized Bibles or prayer books specifically suited for the occasion all make meaningful gifts. Also appreciated are savings bonds, a charitable donation, or even a gift certificate. From crystal angels to collectible figurines, there's something special for every meaningful religious event.

T

Is for Thank-you Gifts

Have you ever received a thank-you note or gift that really made you feel appreciated and special? Whenever I am sent one, I save it and over the years have filled a special box with words that I read often to brighten my day. These thank-you notes and tokens of affection are also gifts. Since words are free and fabulous, they are there for the choosing. In fact, the power of a thank you has limitless possibilities and makes everyone feel good.

Saying "thank you" is in good taste. It's also meaningful and can become a lasting memory. Of course, it takes time and energy to write thank-you notes, but they mean so much to the recipient and do not have to be a chore. Be clever, be original, and make the person you're thanking know that you are really grateful. Be prepared to say thank you and have special stationery you enjoy sending and a few thank-you gifts on hand. If you can make your gift reflect what you are thanking someone for, you'll double its impact.

Here are some ways to help you express your thanks with style.

Clever Thank Yous— Wake Up Your Words!

When someone gives you a gift, be specific and acknowledge what he or she gave you. Be creative and have fun by saying thank you with a play on words. Here are some clever examples to combine with your heartfelt thanks.

Antique—"The antique silver spoon you selected will be treasured for many more years to come. Your good taste is reflected in your beautiful gift, and old is gold in my book!"

Art—"Like the beautiful painting you chose for us, you are one of a kind—and very kind to us, I might add!"

Baby gift—"Your pink hand-knitted sweater [blanket, etc.] welcomed our bundle of joy with such warmth and generosity. You must be a mind reader, since we were hoping for a handmade treasure made with love from you."

Book—"As friends go, you're a best-seller! Leave it to you to make such a novel choice! Thank you for sharing this special chapter in my life."

Camera—"Picture me smiling! Your gift was exactly what I wanted for my birthday. I love taking photographs and thanks to you I have the coolest camera on earth. Thank you for a picture-perfect present."

Candy—"Thank you for the delicious gourmet chocolates. The only thing sweeter than this gift is you!"

Charitable Donation—"Thank you for a gift that makes a difference to others. I admire and value the work that [the charity] is doing. Be assured, you make a big difference to us, too."

Clothing—"You know I have a passion for fashion and thanks to you your gift will keep me up-to-date and in style. Every time I get a compliment on my new [name item], I'll be thinking of my cousins who have

such great taste and made me look good."

Crystal—"It's crystal clear you have great taste. Thank you for the lovely [name item]. It will be enjoyed at many happy occasions, and we'll think of you each and every time we use it."

Easter—"Thank you so much for the Easter basket. I've never seen such an 'egg-stravagant' assortment of candy and lovingly colored Easter eggs in my whole life."

Flowers—"The floral fantasy you sent was exquisite. The display of flowers brightened my day upon their arrival and made me feel like queen for a day."

Food Gift—"Your [name gift] was not only edible, but incredible, just like you. Thank you for your good taste and a gift that sure tasted good!"

Hospitality—"Thank you so much for your hospitality. In just two days, you made me feel like a welcomed part of your family and right at home also."

Jewelry—"Thank you for being a jewel of a friend. Your beautiful [name gift] are [is] priceless to me, just like our friendship."

Kitchen—"You certainly are a kitchen magician. It's magic to see what you conjure up with just a few ingredients. Thank you for the tasty treats."

Money—"I cannot tell a lie. All those George Washington bills made my day. Both my wallet and I say thank you!"

Photography—"The pictures you took at [name event] are magnificent. Thank you so much for arranging them into the lovely album, and thank you for being such a straight shooter as my best friend."

Scented Gift—"Thank you for the 'scent-sational' gift."

Toy—"My eyes almost popped out when I saw my new [name toy]. You must be a mind reader since I've been bugging my parents for it. You sure know the way to a kid's heart."

Watch—"It's about time I said thank you for being such a good friend."

Thank-you Gifts

Just Say Thanks. Create personalized stationery or lovely notecards, just in time for those after-holiday or emergency thank yous. Consider photocopying your children's artwork for instant notecards printed on card-stock paper. Tie a ribbon around the cards and envelopes for a meaningful gift. Or, if you're a computer whiz,

create some designer stationery with her name and address, and print out an assortment of personalized papers.

A Notable Thanks. When someone has done a great job at a specific task, send a box of pretty notecards and a matching pen, with a card saying, "Your hard work is notable!"

Books They'll Be Thankful For. Check out my book *The Thank You Book*, and for kids be sure to get a copy of teen author Ali Spizman's book *The Thank You Book for Kids*. Ali's goal was to inspire other kids to express kindness, and this book is a how-to guide for writing meaningful thank yous. A must-have for the coolest kids as well as the thank-you impaired.

You're A-1 with Me. Did he organize a terrific meeting? Send him a box of steaks with a bottle of A-1 Sauce®. Or just pour on the sauce and send sauces. Add a note that says, "You're A-1 with me!"

You Nailed It! If she did a fabulous job on a project, whether at work or helping you wallpaper a room, give her a gift certificate for a manicure, with a note exclaim-

Thank-you words to choose and use

amazing	tasteful	dazzling
terrific	chic	awesome
classy	flair	stunning
devine	in vogue	sumptuous
elegant	the rage	unforgettable
outrageous	fabulous	magnificent
over the top	breathtaking	monumental
pizzazz	splendid	superb
tempting	knockout	irresistible
special	exquisite	picture-perfect
first-rate	first-class	incomparable
surpasses	the finest	outshines
supreme	impeccable	unparalleled
stylish	dashing	distinctive

ing, "You really nailed that one! Thanks."

You Hammered That One Home! He had a huge success with a project. Send him a hammer and a selection of nails from the hardware store with a note, "Thanks. You hammered that one home!" Hand-paint the hammer for a fashionable statement for women with polka dots or leopard spots, or paint a handle with a sporting theme like black-and-white referee stripes for dad. The kids will love helping transform ordinary, inexpensive hammers into works of art.

Snack Attack. If someone put in long hours on your behalf or the going is tough, drop off a "snack attack," a shopping bag filled with munchies, fruit, and soft drinks.

Magnetic Personality. Did an employee do a superb job and help improve the bottom line? Give her a box of clever refrigerator magnets with a card, "We attract more business thanks to you!"

Prince Charming. He came to your rescue and saved the day. Send him a one-time-use camera, a coupon for developing film, and a photo album or a framed photograph of him. Add a note that says, "Thanks to my 'prints' charming."

Sweet Dreams. Arrive as a houseguest armed with a gracious way to say "thank you." Bring along a small token of your affection, ranging from a stylish alarm clock to a bedside magnifying mirror, and before you make your departure, tuck the gift next to your hostess's pillow with a note, "Sweet dreams to the perfect hostess."

Hanging Around. When you're a guest in someone's home, leave a gift in the guest room for the pleasure of the next guest: several pretty, decorated hangers in the closet with a note for the hostess, "I just loved hanging around with you."

You Wrote the Book. Say "thank you" after being a guest with a copy of a new novel or a book about your host's passionate hobby. Include a card, "You wrote the book on hospitality."

Magazine Scene. After a stay as a houseguest, leave a current copy of an interesting magazine on the nightstand. Leave a note saying,

"You deserve a break! This is the first of many. I've entered a subscription in your name for a year's worth of good reading."

Let Me Entertain You. If someone treated you to dinner at a restaurant and you wish to reciprocate in a creative way, send your host or hostess a thank-you note with a menu of choices and a reciprocal invitation to join you for dinner. Add these words, "I had such a marvelous time at dinner, now let me entertain you! Choose the date and restaurant from this menu and please RSVP to me."

Stuck on You. It was a tough job, but they followed it through to the end. Say thank you with a bag full of "sticky" gifts: colorful Post-It notes, glue, tape, personalized address stickers, sticky candy, and say, "Thanks for sticking with me" or "Wish you could stick around longer! Thank you for your help."

See the Light. Send an encouraging thank you with a scented candle for work well done to encourage completion of a task: "Thanks to your hard work, we can see the light at the end of the tunnel."

A Gold Mine. When someone has offered you great advice, or helped you work through a dilemma, send a gift of gold . . . real gold jewelry if you can afford it, gold-wrapped candy nuggets otherwise, with a note saying, "I struck gold when I met you!"

Out of a Jam. If you were really stuck, and a friend stepped forward with help, send a gift basket with a jar of jam, a loaf of bread, and a note, "Thanks so much for getting me out of a jam."

Hugs and Kisses. Take a camera to a wedding or other festive event. Capture the celebrants hugging and kissing. Make up a photo album of these prints and present it to the hosts with an inscription, "Your party was picture-perfect!" Or, "Hugs and kisses to you! We had a fabulous time!"

A Friend in "Knead." When a friend has helped you and you wish to send a humorous thanks, send a loaf of bread or splurge and send a bread machine with the words, "Thank you for being there in my hour of 'knead.' "

Thanks for the Memories. Your friends just threw you a birthday or anniversary party. Thank them by assembling a photo album of pic-

tures of the bunch of you through the years. Add anecdotes and memories, and send it with a note, "Thanks for all the memories."

A Penny for Your Thoughts. Tell her if you gave her a penny for every time she'd been thoughtful to you, you'd owe her a million bucks. Say thanks for her help and good thoughts with a pretty box filled to the brim with shiny new pennies.

Peachy Keen. Say thank you for a friend's thoughtfulness with a basket of peaches, "You're a real peach." Out of season? Send a peach pie or jar of peach preserves with the same sentiment.

Ready, Willing, and "Label." If a friend's lent a hand for a big job, like a garage sale or room renovation, send personalized stationery and return address labels, stamps and a pen, with a note, "Thanks for being ready, willing, and "label" to help me."

Shower Them with Thanks. Say thank you with a colorful umbrella and a quick note, "Rain or shine, we're pouring on the thanks!" Or, "Showering you with endless thanks."

Thank-you Box. A treasure box filled with thank-you gifts is a great way to say "thank you" to a child for a job well done or an act of kindness or consideration. Fill the box with small treasures you know the child will like: trading cards, model cars, stickers, candy, a book. Include a note, "Your behavior was a treasure—and so are you!"

Lollipop, Lollipop. Send one huge lollipop or a gift bag full of different flavors with a note, "I'd be a real sucker not to thank you for everything you've done for me." Or, "Popping in to say thanks."

Meant to Mentor. Did someone give you a lead on a job? Make a call to get you an interview? Send a box of mints with a note, "Thanks for being my mentor. You were 'mint' for the job."

VIP Voluteers. Say "thank you" to volunteers or coworkers with a bag of bubblegum wrapped up with a pretty bow. Add a note that says, "I'd 'chews' to work with you any time."

Thank-You Note Jump-Starts

Use the following sentences to jump-start your heartfelt thanks:

Anniversary

"When you've been married as long as we have, there are few surprises left in life. But we were surprised and deeply touched by your most thoughtful gift and incredible party. We will remember it, and you, forever. Thank you for the memory of a lifetime."

"Your scrapbook of mementos from the wedding reminded us how friends like you are pure gold. What a delight it was to have the opportunity to share happy times together."

"We send our deepest thanks and appreciation for giving us your presence in our lives and such a fabulous gift as well."

Thank You for the Gift

"Thank you for your very generous gift. I couldn't believe my eyes when I opened your beautifully wrapped package. How did you ever know that [name the gift] would be precisely what I would have chosen for myself? I can't begin to tell you how I appreciate having a friend like you and, once again, my sincerest thanks."

"How can I ever thank you for your lovely gift? Its presence will brighten my home as your presence brightens my days. It truly is a joy counting you among my dearest friends, and I look forward to sharing many happy times ahead."

"What a thoughtful welcome you sent our precious baby daughter, [name of child] upon her arrival. The pink-and-white party dress with the appliquéd rabbit instantly put a smile on all of our faces. [Name of child] will be ready to celebrate many happy occasions in style thanks to your excellent choice of gifts."

Thank You, Family

"What did I ever do to deserve parents like you? I know I never said it often enough growing up, but thank you from the bottom of my heart. You've done so much for me my entire life, and once again the gift of your presence and guidance is the very best gift of all."

"Somebody once said you can pick your friends, but you can't pick your family. Well, if I had the whole world to pick from, I'd choose you first. Thank you so much for your thoughtful gift!"

"We must be related. Nobody else could ever read my mind so

clearly and come up with exactly what I wanted for my birthday."

"Thank you for caring today and every day about our happiness. We are the luckiest parents on earth to have a child like you."

Thank You, Friends

"Robert Louis Stevenson said, 'A friend is a gift you give yourself.' In our case, that's so true! You are definitely one of the best gifts life has to offer. I feel so lucky that you are my friend. Your friendship is the most meaningful gift I could ever receive."

"You're more than a friend, you're my alter ego and best friend for life. Which must be how you knew what to choose for my birthday. The [name of gift] is absolutely perfect, and so are you. Thank you so much, not just for my gift, but for being in my life. Thank you for being the world's best friend and having such a generous heart."

"I knew my ship would come in someday, but I didn't know it would be a friendship that made me rich in all the ways that matter most. You are such a blessing to me, and I am so fortunate to call you my friend."

Thanks for the Good Wishes

"I did it! With the help and support of all my friends and family, I graduated. Thanks for being there in so many ways. And thank you for your most generous check. It will help give me a head start on the road to college."

"My endless thanks for your kind words and the [name of gift]. Your good wishes continue to reflect on your love and concern for my well-being. You mean the world to me, and I send my deepest thanks for your continued support."

Thank You, Grandparents

"Grandma and Grandpa, you've got to be the world's best grandparents. I wish you could have been here when I opened your present. I actually did a backflip over the [name of gift], and your gift took my breath away. It is so cool to have grandparents who can read my mind. I can't wait for you to visit, and I hope to see you soon. Your gift was awesome, just like you both!"

"Grandma and Grandpa, Mommy is writing this for me, but I am telling her what to say. The doll you sent me is going to be my very favorite. Her skin feels as soft as my new little brother's, and she cries louder than he does. I love her so much, but I love you most of all!"

Thank You for Thinking of Me

"There are some situations where words aren't enough to express emotion, and this is one of them. You were a total lifesaver while I was ill. I don't know how my family could have survived without your support, your days spent shopping for me, driving carpool, cooking, and cleaning. How can I ever thank you enough for being there for all of us in a trying time?"

"It's no puzzle why you are so wonderful. You kept my spirits high while I was feeling low. Thank you for thinking of me."

Kids Thanks

"Thank you so much for coming to my birthday party. I hope you had as much fun as I did, and your gift was the icing on the cake and made my day. The [name of gift] you gave me was a first-prize present, and I feel like I won the gift lottery thanks to you! I hope to see you soon so that I can thank you in person."

"Mom and Dad, you are the greatest. I'm sitting here in my dorm room, looking at all the neat stuff you surprised me with. I never expected to have a [name(s) of gift(s)] at college. Thank you so much. But thank you so much more for inspiring me, making sure I studied and did well enough in high school to make it to college in the first place. I am grateful for everything you have done and for loving me like you do."

Mentor/Teacher

"Now that I'm graduating, I can look back at my school days and see that of all the wonderful gifts I've received, yours was the best. You took the time to make me realize that not only do I love to learn, but I am good at it. You encouraged me when things got tough, and thanks to you, I now have a firm foundation to build on as I begin college. Thanks so much for the love of learning you instilled in me."

"What is a mentor? If it's someone who takes your hand, guides you over the rough spots, and helps shape you into a success, then you earn the title as my mentor, and I thank you from the bottom of my heart. You gave me direction when I was lost and instruction when I needed it most. You helped me find myself and determine my path for my future. You gave me the gift of your time and expertise, and for this I will be forever grateful."

Thank You, Volunteers

"Thank you beyond words for your most generous check. Your contribution will make a big difference to our entire organization. You can be proud of supporting a worthy cause, and we are very grateful for your support."

"Thank you for being a volunteer. I know it can be a thankless job with long hours, no pay, no real guidelines, and often no help. But the results are well worth it, and I thank you especially for your help and encouragement that have kept me going, too, when things got to be too much."

Wedding Thank Yous

"My wedding wouldn't have been nearly as perfect without you by my side as my maid of honor. Thank you for all that you did: the world's best shower, the hilarious video at the rehearsal dinner, all the help getting me stuffed into my gown, and the makeup repair after the ceremony. You are a treasure in my life, and I feel so fortunate we are friends."

"Thank you so much for the generous gift of a [name gift]. This gift really registered with us! It was the perfect choice, and we will always remember you cared enough to send us something we really wanted and needed. I am so sorry you couldn't be with us for the wedding. Your absence was certainly felt, and your thoughtful gift will always be appreciated."

"Thank you so much for the [name gift]. When we get back from our honeymoon, you'll have to come over and have dinner. We were so happy you were able to make it to the wedding. It wouldn't have been the same without you, and we cherished your presence more than you'll ever know."

U

Is for Unique Gifts

When you want to make a statement, give a gift that screams, "You're special!" to the recipient. Unique gifts should be memorable and can range in price from zero to the sky's the limit. In this case, it's the thought that counts, but sometimes that also means accompanying it is a hefty price tag. The key to being unique is to think carefully about the person you're giving the gift to. That doesn't mean you have to spend a small fortune. On the other hand, you just might need a bank loan for a few of these.

Begin by focusing on his likes and dislikes, her passions and talents, and try to find just that perfect gift that nobody else has thought of before. Sometimes it's as easy as adding his or her initials, and other times it's staying up on the trends and latest gadgets. Before long, they'll think you're a gift-giving pro, so don't give up. Asks lots of questions of sales people, and shop until you find that gift as unique as your favorite friend or your one-of-a-kind relative!

Fruit of the Vine. Give the wine lover an excellent bottle of vintage wine from a famous vineyard. Search for a bottle of the same year they got married, or perhaps a bottle that is his same age (or age he wishes he was!). For an informed connoisseur, find out distinct preferences and inquire about personalized labels available through specialty wineshops for a way to commemorate a special occasion or your sentiment.

First Edition. Find out his favorite author or book from childhood, and purchase a first-edition volume. Add a note (don't write in the book, that will decrease its value), "In my book, you'll always be a first edition!"

Car Crazy. If he loves his car more than any possession on earth, then drive him crazy with a luxury item such as a custom-made steering wheel, a year's worth of detailing at his garage, new hub caps, a personalized license plate, or something useful that will enhance his car's value and he'll really appreciate. At a loss for what to give? Just find out his mechanic's name, and you'll have a good head start.

Oldie but Goldie. Search antique shops for a one-of-a-kind antique piece of jewelry. Do a little research and find what era it's from and any history that might be relevant or interesting. From cameos, to deco stickpins, to Victorian sweetheart bracelets, there's a world of interesting styles and choices. Present the information with a card that says, "To a real jewel" or "There's no friend like an old friend."

Member of the Club. Give an individual or a family a membership to their local art museum, theater, zoo, history center, or something that reflects his or her interests. This is a wonderful way to get involved in the community and will save them money year round as well. You can also give memberships to special shopping clubs, warehouse stores, or dining-out clubs that they would really enjoy. Add a note that says, "A VIP membership for a VIP friend (or family)."

G.I. Joe. Personalized dog tags are a unique gift for anyone. They are perfect for kids going off to camp or even for the family pet. For an adult, think 14k gold or sterling silver for a campy, yet practical, gift. All you need is their name, rank (first-class kid) and serial number (birth date). This is also a meaningful keepsake for dating partners with their names together along with the anniversary of their first date.

Man (Woman or Child) of the Year. Have a magazine cover printed with his or her photo. You can do this yourself and paste it up at a quick copy store or on your computer. Include their face, alter the headline, and have it framed handsomely for a really unique gift to put on a desk or hang in a den.

Pocket Perfect. Everybody's got a pocketknife, but how about one that does everything but cook dinner for you? For the handyman, the outdoorsman, the hiker or camper, the traveler, you can't do better than offer a handy, all-inclusive, do-everything knife.

Gadget Mania. You think you've seen everything? How about a cell phone combined with a digital camera, a digital camera the size of a pen, or a combination DVD, VCR, and TV all in one? Gadget lovers flip over those conversation pieces and high-tech toys. Check out wristwatches that double as cameras and other cool gifts. There's something for everyone when it comes to gadgets.

For the Birds. If you know someone who's a bird lover, indulge her passion. Start with a pair of binoculars or a telescope, a book to help identify birds, and a notebook to record sightings. And don't forget the birds. Include a personalized birdhouse with the family name on it and lots of birdseed to attract happy customers for close-up viewing.

Starry, Starry Night. A stargazer's fantasy, offer a course in astronomy along with a telescope powerful enough to pierce the heavens. This is an enlightened gift for your favorite superstar. Add a note that says, "No one shines brighter than you!"

Mastering the Art. Enrich a friend's life with gourmet-cooking lessons, either in a class or one-on-one with your city's finest chef. Announce the gift with an apron, a chef's hat, and a set of excellent knives, a new pot or pan or kitchen gadget she or he will enjoy.

Someone's in the Kitchen. If they lead a busy life with no time to cook, hire a personal chef, someone who'll come in daily or weekly and cook up a storm, leaving your gift recipient gourmet delicacies for each night's dinner. Many personal chefs will do the shopping, too, and coordinate the gift recipient's likes and dislikes. Pay for some freezer pleasers as well to be left in disposable containers for an added touch.

H_2O to Go. For the busy, home-based executive or sports fan who drinks tons of water, order an at-home water-cooler dispenser and a year's worth of refills. Add a note that says, "To one cool friend!"

What's Up, Doc? Dr. Kildare never made the fashion statement your medical professional will make in custom-made scrubs. You can choose the color, the fabric, the cut, and make him or her stand out from the crowd in the OR.

Where There's a Will. Or where there isn't one. Everyone should be covered by a valid will. If you know someone who isn't, the gift of a lawyer's time and effort to draw up a will is one of the most thoughtful gifts you can give.

Designer on Call. If the house is a wreck, but she's just too busy to redecorate, offer her the help of an interior designer. Be sure to choose one whose style is compatible with hers. "Paint and paper and furniture, too, this designer will give you a look that's new." Or if you've got the touch, offer a day of your time for furniture rearranging and picture hanging.

When the Spirits Move. Hire a Feng Shui specialist to come in and do a reading for a friend. They'll find out how to reposition furnishings to maximize the positive energy in his or her surroundings with this Asian technique.

Cool Hand Luke. If he fancies himself a pool shark, treat him to his own custom-made, personalized pool cue and carrying case.

Taster's Choice. A gourmet's dream. Treat a friend to a "progressive" dinner beginning with hor d'oeurvres at one restaurant, the main course at the next one, and so on. Include a variety of eating styles ranging from fine dining, ethnic, casual, to specialty eateries.

Future Focus. If you want to give a special gift to a person who believes in ESP and other related areas, make an appointment to have her aura read. Give her a cleansing crystal, or if she's game, a reading from a local psychic.

Fantasy on Wheels. You can't make all his fantasies come true, but here's one you can fulfill. Rent him his dream car for a day. Whether it's a Rolls Royce, Ferrari, or an antique T-Bird, have it roll up to his door early in the morning. Have laid out on the seat a jaunty British driving cap, a pair of leather driving gloves, and a note that says, "This 'auto' keep you happy for a while!"

The Kindest Words. Give the gift of beauty for her written words. Search out fine, handmade paper crafted into notes and envelopes. Include a vintage fountain pen and ink, or a beautiful pen to coordinate with the paper. Add your heartfelt feelings, roll it, and tie it up with a colorful ribbon.

In Their Honor. If money is no object, think of honoring a special someone by naming a building, a floor, or a wing after him. You might choose a hospital, a school or college, a group home, or charity-based organization. Or endow a chair at a university, giving eternal honor to them.

The Name Game. On a more humorous scale, if they are regulars at a restaurant, see if you can have a nameplate put on their favorite booth, or arrange for their photograph to be added to the wall of a famous restaurant they frequent.

Party Hearty. Surprise a friend with an extravagant party in his or her honor. An evening of jazz music at a local nightclub, a moonlit cruise, a night of dancing under the stars in a rooftop lounge, a formal ball in a swanky ballroom, a big campout with hotdogs and marshmallow toasting. Tailor the party to their taste, and invite everyone they care about. Make them the star of the evening, with music, toasts, a retrospective video show, and personalized party favors featuring the guest of honor.

A Cyber-Search. If someone or their company is in the news a great deal, consider doing a search online and printing out a collection of all the articles of interest you can find. Have the pages bound into a book and create a cover page that says, "This is your (cyber) life!"

Come Fly Away. Probably the most awesome, unique gift you can give is a trip to Paradise, whatever your giftee's idea of Paradise is. Perhaps it's a week on a lazy Hawaiian island (the Fiftieth state for a Fiftieth birthday or anniversary?). Announce it with a fresh pineapple and orchids. Perhaps it's a Greek island, tell them with ouzo and moussaka. Paris? Rome? Tokyo? Find a great travel agent to help you plan every aspect of the trip, from transportation to and from the airport to the flight, hotels, meals, sightseeing, even souvenirs and shopping sprees if you choose. Don't forget to give them good lightweight luggage and a digital camera, plus a limited-time international cell phone or prepaid phone card to stay in touch while they're gone.

See Food...Seafood. If they are seafood lovers, arrange to have a seafood company send their favorite delicacy through the mail. Search online for the best companies who specialize in mail-order seafood. When they *see* this food, they'll thank you!

Initially Speaking. From monogrammed linen cocktail napkins to a cashmere scarf, the gift of personalization continues to be a winner. Think out of the box and have his favorite shirt or her throw monogrammed, or consider having a famous quote or words like *Dream, Believe* or *My Beloved* embroidered on a pillow. This is also ideal for a new arrival with baby's name and birth date.

Fly Me to the Moon. Well, not exactly the moon, but from New York you can be in London in three hours and fifty minutes on the supersonic Concorde. Be sure to book tickets ahead of time for a few shows, and while you are there see the Tower of London and the changing of the guard, and maybe take the "chunnel" across to France for an afternoon of shopping in Paris. If you're into history, take a day to visit Stonehenge. You'll be flying high with the excitement of this trip.

Championship Point. Give him a digital camera and an envelope. He'll know he's scored a win when he opens it to find tickets to the Super Bowl, the World Series, the NBA Finals, the U.S. Open Golf Tournament, or the U.S. Open Tennis Championships. Include an IOU for airline tickets and hotel reservations, which you can't confirm in some events until the teams are chosen. Add a note, "I am a winner for teaming up with you."

Paris in the Springtime. Paris means romance. Stroll down the broad avenues, and visit the museums. You'll be all smiles when you view the *Mona Lisa*! Dine under the stars and wander the Left Bank, stopping to visit Picasso's home and the quaint shops that crowd the area. Keep your head when you visit Versailles, home of Marie Antoinette. And don't forget to bring home some French perfume and a tin of truffles.

Clearly Special. Some things are so special, you just have to own at least one. From handblown glass by a famous artist to something fragile from a legendary store, make it clear you care about someone when you present a gorgeous piece of timeless glass. Add a note that says, "It's clear we were meant to be together" or "It's crystal clear we'll be friends forever."

I'll Take Manhattan. Make your New York getaway an affair to remember. First, a limo from the airport to your hotel. A buggy ride through Central Park. Take a taxi to Chinatown and walk from there back up Broadway, stopping for dim sum, then ice cream, and a side trip for pickles and a bit of Lower East Side bargain hunting. Back uptown for dinner and a show. New York may be neither *new* nor *York*, but it certainly is the city that never sleeps, and you won't want to miss one minute of your time there, either.

Auction Fever. If you're in the New York area, look at the schedules for auctions. Pick one you're passionate about and attend. Even if you can't afford much, you'll enjoy the fun of viewing the items up for bid, and the excitement and drama of the auction itself, with the subtle bids from regulars, the tension as an item gets bid up far beyond expectations, and the joy when someone wins a bid. Good luck and good bidding to you. Give your companion the news about the big day by writing it in the form of an invitation on a bidding paddle. "On Monday, you and I will be going, going, gone to a rare-book auction, so save the date!"

A Hole-in-One Gift. If he's a serious golfer, then he'll flip over playing golf at any of the most famous golf courses in the world. From weekend getaways at nearby courses to faraway places he's only dreamed about, give him a trip to play golf on the greens of his dreams.

Tour De France. You've been to Paris, seen the Riviera, now experience the real France. Arrange a bicycle trip or rent a house for a few weeks in Provence, just long enough to sample the restaurants in the tiny villages surrounding you. If you're very lucky, you might be able to sign up for a cooking course from a top-notch chef. If not, just enjoy the cuisine while you can. I dare you to return home without a single charming antique.

Remote Possibilities. Does the love of your life love his remote controls as much as he loves you? Buy him a roomful of advanced electronics: a home-theater system, a huge screen TV, DVD player, state-of-the-art stereo system with AM/FM/short wave radio, CD and tuner for his old records, a satellite system for the TV, an intercom to connect him to the rest of the house, and an up-to-date computer system with cordless mouse so he can lounge as he surfs the net. Plus, don't forget a high-tech remote control that consolidates his beloved toys!

Coming Clean. Send her off to a luxury spa for the weekend. Announce the gift with a basket of sensual body oils and scrubs. When she gets home, completely decorate her bathroom with candlelight, wine chilling and soft music playing, and flowers floating in the water.

Starring . . . Him. Get him a gig with his favorite group, especially if that group is the local symphony orchestra. Arrange for him to guest conduct at a free concert or rehearsal. Make up invitations in the form of a concert program, and invite friends to join you for the gala event, including a post-concert supper, of course.

Safe and Sound. Give him his own fireproof vault where he can put his papers, jewels, or stash some cash. There are several sizes, so be sure to check this one out with him first to get his approval. Then have it delivered to his home or office and installed in a safe hiding place. This will be one gift that lasts a lifetime.

Quirky Collectibles. Find out what she collects and give an addition to her collection. From Elvis memorabilia, spoons, antique toys, Victorian dresser jars, china boxes, tea cups, salt shakers, to vintage post cards. Once you have insider's information on her favorite things, you can select a unique gift that will be a welcomed addition to her prized collection.

The Fast Lane. If he loves boats, trains, planes, even go-carts, or anything that's high performance and over the top, he'll love a book or magazine subscription that features the crème de la crème. Or, research and give him an all-expense-paid trip to one of the classic car or top racing events. Include a book on high-performance vehicles that are state-of-the-art and throw in a gift certificate for a new set of those high-performance tires he's always wanted for a gift that will drive him wild. Also, throw in a few computer games that simulate high-speed racing so he can try his hand at the wheel.

V

Is for Valentine and Romantic Gifts

What could possibly be more fun than choosing valentine's and gifts for the one you love? Valentine's Day is the eternal day for lovers and significant others, but the key is to make this day of heartfelt expression spill over into the rest of the year. Let Valentine's Day be your diving board for love into the other 364 days of the year. Express your affection when someone is least likely to expect it and celebrate your relationship year round.

Here's an area where you can let your imagination run wild, let the prose get hot and heavy, the selections sweet and sensuous. Learn how to say "I love you" in a million small and big ways, and you've got it made!

It's Only Puppy Love. Tell her it's more than puppy love and present her with a stuffed puppy on the anniversary of your first date together. For a memorable touch, hang a special piece of jewelry around its collar or attach a beauti-

ful pin to it. No doghouse for you tonight!

The "Write" Start. Give a journal to your special someone on the anniversary of your first date. Write your feelings of what she or he means to you on the first page and then it's his or her turn to write the next entry. Pass the book back and forth and share how you cherish this important date and each other, month-by-month or whenever the mood strikes.

Déjà Vu. Re-create the night you first met. Call your sweetheart and ask him or her out on a date. Rent a vintage auto reminiscent of the one you drove on that first special evening together. Visit the places you went, order burgers and fries at your old hangout, if possible. Roll out the golden oldies and make it a night to remember, again and again. And don't forget to be as head-over-heels in love as you were at the very start!

Sealed with a Kiss. Snap a photograph of the happy couple kissing. Frame a copy, and it will be a special moment frozen in time that will last a lifetime.

My One and Only. Less is more in this case. Send your true love a single rose in a bud vase. Add the note, "You are my one and only."

Sweeten the Moment. Transform a box of chocolates into a romantic gesture by hiding a piece of jewelry in the box. Remove one bon-bon and replace it with a necklace, ring, or bracelet. She'll think it's just candy and have the surprise of a lifetime when she opens the box. This is a memorable way to pop the question!

A Latte for Your Hot-ee! Give a gift filled with flavored coffees, a gift card to his favorite coffee house, or a mug of hot coffee with a little note that says, "A cup of latte for my favorite hot-ee!"

"Eye" Love You! Tell her, "I only have eyes for you" and give her a new pair of sunglasses, magnifying glasses, or a beautiful case for her glasses. The choices are endless, and your tasteful gift will be eye-catching. A useful way to tell someone, "Eye love [adore, admire, respect] you!"

Bombard Your Valentine. Don't send a Valentine card. Send dozens, including the dime-store ones like my father did when he gave my mother an entire box, one-by-one! Stock up on funny ones, mushy romantic ones, serious ones, poetry, cartoons, lace. Send some through the mail, some in e-mail. Hide some in her drawers and tuck them under her pillow. Slide them inside the newspaper and scatter them on the couch. Overwhelm her with loving thoughts that all say, "Be mine."

A to Z. The romantically inclined would agree that yearly traditions create something special to look forward to in order to add some fun. Choose a restaurant to eat at on Valentine's Day that begins with the letter *A* and then work (eat) your way through the alphabet. Move to the next letter in case you get stumped, and start over when you get to *Z*.

Can't Bear to Be Without Her? Find your valentine a plush, cuddly teddy bear. Present it with a note, "I can't bear to be without you." Be sure to follow up with a bear hug of your own!

A **Designer Kiss.** Search for a lipstick shade that symbolizes your love. For example, check out the names of the colors that range from guy's and girl's names to words of love like *dream*, *forever*, and *passion*. You'll be surprised how much this gift is appreciated and don't forget to seal it with a kiss, from you, of course!

Cupid, Draw Back Your Bow. Cupid is the symbol of love, the naughty boy whose arrows pierce deep into the heart, making you fall in love. Give your love a Cupid statue and a note that says, "Cupid knew what he was doing when he hit us with his arrow!"

The Way to a Man's Heart. Don't give him a box of chocolates for Valentine's Day. Come prepared to make your own dessert. Bring along a bag of ingredients to make your own chocolate creations. There is no substitute for the perfect chocolate cake for a sinful sensation.

You Are My Fortune. Give her a box of fortune cookies with the ultimate expression of love that declares, "No message needed, you are my fortune."

Music for Her Ears. Record or select a CD of your love's favorite love songs and pop it into the car CD player. When she starts the car to go to work or drive in her carpool and turns on the CD player, your words of love will turn on, too. Choose from *I Just Called to Say I Love You*, to *Love Me Tender*, to vintage Sinatra, to *He's So Fine*, and even *Dedicated to the One I Love*.

Back and Forth. With a video-camera, go back and forth asking each other questions about how you met. What did he love about you most? When was the first time she knew she loved you? What does he remember about proposing to you? This tape will be a treasured memory, perfect for watching each anniversary to come.

Secret Code. Have a special code that means "I Love You" that only the two of you understand. For example, send the numbers 4, 5, and 9 which correspond with the letters *I, L,* and *Y* on a telephone or cell phone.

Stretch Your Point. Get across how much you love her by picking her up in a stretch limo for a surprise date. Fill the car with little gifts that you pull out all night long, and maximize your message of love.

"Mint" for Each Other. Fill a bag or box with his or her favorite flavor of mints and add a note that says, "We were mint for each other."

Magnetic Attraction. Buy a set of refrigerator magnet letters and spell out I LOVE YOU FOREVER on his refrigerator.

The Language of Love. Learn to say "I love you" in a number of foreign languages. Here are a few to get you started:

Afrikaans: *Ek is life vir jou.*
Bengali: *Ami tomake bahlobashi.*
Danish: *Jeg elsker dig.*
Dutch: *Ik hou van je.*
French: *Je t'aime.*
German: *Ich liebe dich.*
Greek: *S'ayapo.*
Hawaiian: *Aloha wau ia 'oe.*
Hebrew: *Ani ohev otakh* (man to woman), *Ani ohevet otkha* (woman to man).
Irish: *t'a gr'a agam dhuit.*
Italian: *Ti amo.*
Japanese: *Kimi o ai shiteru.*
Mandarin: *Wo ai ni.*
Portuguese: *Eu te amo.*
Russian: *Ya tyebya lyublyu.*

Spanish: *Te amo.*
Swahili: *Nakupenda.*
Turkish: *Seni seviyorum.*
Yiddish: *Kh'hob dikh lib.*
Zulu: *Ngiyakuthanda.*

Message in a Bottle. Send the message loud and clear with a copy of the CD that has *Time in a Bottle* by Jim Croce and a bottle filled with sentiments. Find a pretty, wide-mouth bottle, and fill it with an assortment of candy kisses and heart-shaped candies. Write loving notes on strips of paper, and mix them into the candy. Add a note that says, "I hope you get the message. . . . I love you!"

On Your Toes. Don't overlook her feet when you're thinking romance. Give her a shoebox filled with treasures for her tootsies: a gift certificate for a pedicure or a reflexology treatment, soothing lotion, silk stockings, and a toe ring. Tell her, "You're perfect from your head to your toes."

Kidnapped for Romance. Whisk your partner away for a romantic weekend at a cozy bed-and-breakfast or the penthouse of a grand luxury hotel. Have a limousine pick you up for the ride. When you arrive, arrange to have straw-berries and cream and a bottle of champagne waiting in your room.

A Heart-y Breakfast. Most every-one loves to be surprised with breakfast in bed. Say "I love you" with heart-shaped pancakes and raspberry syrup, fresh berries, and delicious just-brewed coffee.

A Ringing Endorsement. Dia-monds are the traditional lan-guage of love. Show her how valuable she is to you with a gift of diamonds. Buy her a hand-some, locking jewelry case, and lock the ring or other diamond jewelry inside. Hand her the key and tell her, "You hold the key to my heart."

Offer Her Anything. But give her a weekend at her favorite spa, where she'll be pampered and refreshed, packed in mud, mani-cured, pedicured, facialed, and fed healthy goodies galore. Celebrate her return with a candlelit dinner for two, or better yet, go with her and indulge your own need for a little pampering.

Wild Thing. Tell your love how crazy you are about him with a copy of Maurice Sendak's *Where the Wild Things Are.* Add a note that says, "I'm just wild about you." Include the CD *Wild Thing* and tell her, "Wild thing, I think I love you!"

Who Loves You, Baby? While vacationing, take a picture of the words *I love you* written inside a heart and drawn with a stick in the sand. This picture will be a mem-ory to last forever. Plus, spread a little love all over the house. When he gets home from work, have the words *I love you* spelled out in clean socks on the bed, in red marker on the front page of the newspaper, and in candy kisses on his placemat at the dinner table.

Fred and Ginger. Give your part-ner the gift of ballroom dancing lessons. Sign up both of you for lessons, and learn the steps of the tango, the samba, the foxtrot, and the waltz. If he's still stuck in the disco era, have fun and enjoy the music. It will lead to togetherness like you've never experienced before as you step out onto a dance floor in front of awed friends.

Shaping Up. Whether your speed is a full gallop or a half-walk, half-jog, exercising together is as healthy for your heart as it is for your relationship. This is a gift you give to your partner and to yourself. Hide an I-love-you card in a spot where she'll find it for an added surprise.

A Big to-Do. In a crazy, hectic world, time with your partner often gets relegated to last place on the to-do list. Give each other the gift of your undivided attention. Set specific times—one evening a week, an hour on the weekend—that is sacred, and use this time to do something fun and romantic, like a walk in the park, shopping for special treats, or whatever moves you.

Is for Wedding and Shower Gifts

Love is in the air, and everyone loves to celebrate a bride and groom. The entire wedding process calls for inventive gifts, beginning with the newly engaged couple to the shower and wedding itself. To help the couple get a super start in life, your first step is to find out where the couple has registered for gifts and let their tastes guide your selection. You don't want to give country crafts to a couple whose preference is ultracontemporary sleek! And they certainly don't need eight fondue pots or a dozen blenders! So think carefully, and choose thoughtfully for a successful gift that does not have to be returned or stored in a gift closet.

Engagement gifts tend to be more personal items that reflect your good wishes. Shower gifts often focus on a particular practical theme, such as kitchen items, or other home-related gifts. Wedding gifts can be anything you think the new couple will enjoy and use. Cash, bonds, and shares of stock are always in good taste as wedding gifts, too. And there's one more category of gifts to be considered: gifts for members of the wedding party, traditionally given by the bride and groom to their bridesmaids and groomsmen.

Weddings present endless gift-giving opportunities, and here are some suggestions to help you rise to the occasion.

Engagement Gifts

Bells Are Ringing. A lovely Irish traditional gift is a small crystal bell for the engaged couple. This is perfect for the bride and groom who are hearing bells ringing.

Tears of Happiness. Have a few handkerchiefs monogrammed with the bride and groom's names and their wedding date. Or, if you are a do-it-yourselfer, add lace around the edges of a plain handkerchief and handpaint it with fabric paint. Send one to the bride and one to her mother with a note that says,

"For tears of happiness, use these." And, don't forget the father of the bride. For dear ole dad, send a copy of the movie *Father of the Bride*.

Here Comes the Bride. Now that she's engaged, she's got to start planning the wedding. Give her a subscription to a bridal magazine. Tell her, "The best laid plans of brides and *their mothers* produce a picture-perfect wedding."

Organization, Inc. Help the couple get organized for the big event with a wedding planner. Make sure you find one with plenty of pockets for pictures and pages for notes. If you like, tuck in a check for a down payment on the honeymoon or as a contribution for their wish list.

The Way We Were. If you're an old friend, gather photos of their dating days, even of their childhoods, and assemble them into a video montage. They can add to this later with photos from their wedding, honeymoon, and future life highlights.

Wedding Keepsakes. In preparation for the wedding, give the bride and groom a personalized sign-in book for guests and a beautiful pen with a plume. Or,

how about a pair of goblets they can use to toast at their wedding with their names and the wedding date etched into the crystal? Add a note that says, "It's crystal clear you are the perfect pair." Start a tradition with this gift. Toast each other at your wedding and then every anniversary that follows!

Picnic for Two. After all the excitement of the engagement, they'll probably want to get away for some quiet time together. Pack them a picnic basket for two, with their favorite cold edibles, a bottle of wine, juicy red strawberries dipped in chocolate, and directions to a beautiful site for their private feast.

Record Keepers. She'll have an easier time keeping track of guests and gifts if you give her a gift journal (don't forget self-stick numbers to identify gifts), and a white, satin-covered, monogrammed guest book for friends and family to record their good wishes at the wedding and reception.

Memory Keeper. Find a pretty velvet box or satin bag, and have it personalized with the bride and groom's names and wedding date. If you make it yourself, be sure to include a silver lining. Encourage the bride-to-be to save her special correspondence or small treasures from her engagement and wedding to put in it.

A Pearl of a Bride. Be traditional, tried and true, and give the bride-to-be the perfect pearl earrings on the occasion of her engagement. Add a note that says, "A perfect pair for a perfect pair."

Shower Gifts

Shower Them with Love. Give a gift that's practical and fun. Monogram a pair of "His" and "Hers" matching bathrobes, luxuriously deep towels, and washcloths, and include a massaging showerhead. Add a note that says, "Showering you with love and good wishes for a long and happy life together."

The Honeymoon Fun-D. Throw a honeymoon shower and have everyone contribute to the couple's honeymoon fund with gift certificates for massages, eating out, debit or gift cards, prepaid telephone cards to call home (just once!), lingerie for her, new luggage for them, or if you're a check writer, just make a contribution to the fun-d.

Take the Cake. Here's an item they'll need for the wedding. Present them with an engraved crystal or silver-plated cake server and knife to cut the wedding cake. Add a note that says, "May you always have your cake and eat it, too!"

Father and Mother of the Bride. Don't forget the guy who's paying the bills. Give the father and mother of the bride a pocket-sized calculator for guess what?

Just in Case. Give a gift of wedding insurance. It covers unforeseen disasters so the newlyweds are not left holding the bill if the power goes out or the florist doesn't show up. Get all the details and make an informed choice with the couple's approval. Add a note that says, "This is one gift we hope you won't need!"

Wedding SOS. Give the bride-to-be an emergency kit for the big day. Find or make a white satin bag, and fill it with things she might need on her wedding day: a needle and white thread, safety pins, an extra pair of stockings, a comb, hair spray, tissues, breath mints, and stain remover for unexpected spills. "Here's a little SOS—just in case!"

The Look of Love. Pamper the bride-to-be with gift certificates for a manicure, pedicure, and a massage in the days before the wedding. Add a selection of indulgent bath and body gels.

What's Cooking? If the new bride is new to the kitchen, offer her a basic cookbook like *The Joy of Cooking*. Add a box of basic kitchen necessities: spatulas, measuring spoons and cups, a rolling pin, a pie pan, roasting pan, and an apron. Include a note that says, "The way to a man's heart is through his stomach, so start the trip with these."

Pots and Panic. If she's never cooked, give her a set of good, nonstick cookware with a note, "Don't panic at the pans. Cooking's really quite easy once you get the hang of it." Include a cookbook for novices.

Wrapped with Love. Give a gift-wrap organizer filled with brightly colored gift wraps, personalized gift stickers with the couple's names, and ribbon and scissors to create a gift-wrapping treasure chest. Add a note that says, "You're a gift to each other!"

Blended Lives. They'll need a blender (but first make sure they don't have one) and mark the moment with a note that says, "You two are the perfect blend." Or, search for a coffee grinder and brewer, all in one, for devoted coffee "lovers."

Recipes for Success. Gather favorite tried-and-true recipes from those guests invited to the shower. Besides a recipe for something to eat, ask guests to add their instructions for a happy life together. Write or type them on index cards, and tuck them into a pretty recipe box with the words, "Here are some recipes for marital success. Phone numbers are included in case you need a pinch of understanding or a dash of help."

Honeymoon Kit. Find out their honeymoon destination and give a lightweight travel bag to take along. Fill it with items they'll need, including a dictionary if they're leaving the country, a passport holder, some sunscreen, and travel-size sundries. Sunhats and sunglasses are optional. If they're going backpacking or biking, you can place the items in a backpack. Add a note that says, "After the wedding, you'll be going, going, gone, but not without the bare necessities."

Clearly Beautiful. Think ahead to the wedding. Give her a glass dome in which to display her cake topper after the wedding. Get the specifics so that it will be a perfect fit. Have it engraved with their names and the wedding date for the icing on the cake.

Bar None. Stock an ice bucket filled with bar accessories and personalized napkins with their married name. Add stirrers and a few cork and bottle toppers for a decorative touch. Include a note that says, "Bar none, you were meant for each other."

Bridesmaid and Groomsman Gifts

For Her. Engraved silver gifts are the traditional favorite. They are durable, and their engraved message is a reminder both of your joy and your bridesmaid's service to you on your big day. Choose an engraved heart-shaped compact, a silver bracelet with an engraved heart charm, or a silver-plated frame holding a photo of both of you.

For Him. Engrave something for him, too, that will be a memorable keepsake. Choices include a money clip, a travel accessory set, a silver-plated pen and pencil set, a

business-card case, monogrammed handkerchiefs, compasses, or cufflinks.

A Thank You in Bloom. Take a photograph of a flower in bloom that replicates one of the flowers in your bouquet. Consider enlarging and transferring it to black and white and then frame it with a large white mat and a complimentary frame for a one of a kind work of art. Add a thank-you note to the back of the frame with a simple poem that expresses your appreciation that reads as follows:

Like a flower is beautiful
Our friendship is too,
And on my wedding day
I am extra-blessed thanks to you!

Treasure Box. For a bridesmaid who is very sentimental and is someone you treasure, give her a beautiful box (jeweled, antique, covered in satin, silver) and include a letter that tells her how much she means to you. For an added touch, include a pair of pearl studs for a "pearl" of a friend. After the wedding, send a photograph of the two of you to keep in the box along with other memories and items she holds close to her heart.

Your Personal Touch. Most brides and grooms prefer gifts they have registered, but if you want to give something they'll clearly remember was from you, check out the items that can be personalized. Perhaps there's a one-of-a-kind item like a silver water pitcher, glasses, or linens that you can have engraved, etched, or monogrammed to add your personal touch.

Preserve the Bouquet. If she just adores her bouquet, offer to help her keep it permanently. Either rescue it and have it preserved by a professional, or have it recreated in silk flowers for her to enjoy throughout her life. Add a note that says:

*Flowers come and flowers go,
but these are special, this
I know. I've tried to make these
blossoms stay, as fresh as on
your wedding day.*

Magic Moments. Create a memory box full of mementos from the happy couple's courtship and wedding. Include a framed copy of the invitations to the wedding and parties thrown in their honor, favors from the showers and wedding, a wedding program, photos of the bride and groom, her garter, his boutonniere, a sample of the rice or birdseed thrown, and a small book in which friends and family have written their memories of the occasion. Save a wrapped piece of wedding cake in your freezer for a first-anniversary surprise for them.

Nights on White Satin. Help them start married life in sensuous luxury with a set of white satin bedsheets. Or, splurge for those major thread-count sheets and have them monogrammed. Be sure to get the specifics of their bed size.

A Perfect Setting. Check out what's on their registry and if it appears they are getting most everything they wished for, investigate the colors of their fine china and select coordinating linen place mats and napkins, and have them monogrammed for a gorgeous gift. Or, choose breakfast place mats for their everyday china in matching colors.

Big Screen Wishes. If the newlyweds are television addicts, get a group of friends or family members to chip in on the big one—a big screen television. Include a few old romantic movies for the young lovers. Add a note that says, "We'll see you at the Super Bowl—right in your living room!"

Straight from Your He-art! With a little homework, you can give a gift they'll appreciate and love forever. Inquire if the bride and groom are antique collectors, or if they prefer modern art. If you know their taste, then select an object of art ranging from a Staffordshire or bronze statue, to modern handblown glass, or a fabulous black-and-white framed photograph. Include a note that says, "Like your love is one of a kind, so is this gift!"

Double Wedding Ring. If they're a traditional couple that loves handcrafted things, have a "double wedding ring" quilt made for them. Its design will always remind them of your thoughtfulness, and its handmade beauty should last for many years.

By Invitation Only. Have a crystal serving plate or sterling silver box engraved with the wedding invitation for a gift they'll cherish forever. Or, have their wedding invitation placed in an engraved frame for a lasting treasure.

A Sharp Gift. Select a set of English tea knives or antique knives with handles made from mother-of-pearl, bakelite, or silver and have the blades of each engraved. Engrave a phrase on each knife, so that when they are displayed in the box, they spell out a sentence such as:

Happiness forever
Tory and Peter
June 10, 1994
Love to you always!

Or, choose a single butter knife and engrave the blade with words like:

Live, love, and laugh
Spreading good wishes
Phyllis and Jack, January 19, 1947

Moving on Up. Most couples are just starting out and some of their favorite gifts will be useful ones. If you know their sofa needs recovering, or you have a resource that makes beautiful drapes and they are in need of window coverings, offer the gift of some makeover magic. Or, see what they need that they didn't register, like telephones for every room in their home or a refrigerator. It might not be what you think is the perfect wedding gift, but if your goal is to please the bride and groom, give them the gift of choice and something really practical.

A Moment in Time. If you are a photo buff, preserve the wedding day with a photo keepsake album. Take pictures all day from morning until night to highlight the actual day they got married. Take behind-the-scenes pictures ranging from the guest sign-in book, everyone getting ready, the front page of the day's newspaper, and even what was served for dessert. In this case, it's the little things that count. Catch those off-the-beaten-path pictures, and fill a photo album that reflects all the hard work and effort that went into planning a picture-perfect event. Add captions to the photographs for a wedding-day keepsake that will forever be treasured.

X

Is for X-tra Special Deliveries and Gift Wraps

 Since first impressions are lasting impressions, the way your gift is presented is very important. Nothing makes a gift more glamorous than a special delivery with pure pizzazz. But that doesn't mean it has to take you loads of time. Thinking up imaginative ways to present gifts to those you care about can be quite challenging, but the more creative the better, and it's actually fun!

When you receive a gift in a pretty package, it reflects time and effort. No matter the cost of the gift, an extraspecial delivery shows how you feel about someone and makes him or her feel so special. From the way in which you deliver a gift to the style in which it is wrapped, the presentation becomes a memory in itself. Below are some ideas to help you add an original twist to your giftgiving and add miles of smiles to your gifts.

The Gift Fairy. One of my favorite things to do when giving out-of-town gifts to special friend's chil-dren is to enclose a card from "The Gift Fairy." It's so much more exciting to receive the fairy's gifts than one from a faraway adult a young child does not know. Their parents will keep your identity top secret, but when the kids are older—fess up!

String Him Along. Take a spool of ribbon or a ball of yarn, and unroll it all over the house. Attach the opposite end of the string to your gift and carefully hide it in a closet, or even on the kitchen table or in the refrigerator! Put the other end of the string on his pillow. Attach it to a note that says, "Follow me and a gift you'll see." This is also a fun treasure hunt to wake up to. Tie it to her reading glasses or nightstand, so she won't miss it.

Blooming with Love. Whether it's an engagement ring, an anniversary diamond watch, or a friendship bracelet, offer it to her attached to a few stems of gorgeous red roses. Tell her, "My love for you is always blooming."

It's in the Bag. Recycle cookie bags and give him a gift wrapped in one of them and tell him, "You're a chip off the old block," or "Here's to a smart cookie!"

I Love You "Beary, Beary" Much. With a safety pin, carefully pierce the ears of a cuddly teddy bear and then insert those diamond studs or earrings that will leave her breathless. Place the bear on her pillow with the words, "I love you *beary* much."

Cool Deliveries. Attach a gift or love letter to the orange juice container in the refrigerator, along with a note, "Orange you glad we're married?" Or, need to butter her up when delivering an apology? Attach your card or letter asking for her forgiveness on a bar or tub of butter. Place it front row center in the refrigerator. She'll definitely get the point!

On the Ball. Tuck a matching pen and pencil set into a tennis-ball can, and tell him, "For someone who is always on the ball." Or, insert jewelry in the can with a note that says, "We have a love that really scores!"

Fill 'Er Up! Think out of the box when giving a suitcase, briefcase, gym-bag purse, golf bag, or anything that can be filled up. Consider it an opportunity to add an element of surprise and pizzazz. For example, fill an overnight bag with adorable PJ's and slippers for a teenager. Or, when giving a purse, include the same number of items or change as her age in a wallet. Give twenty ones for a teenager who is turning twenty or fifty packs of gum for the fifty-year-old. Or, consider lipsticks in a purse for every day of the week, or fill sport bags with running socks, energy bars, golf balls or basketballs, or sports towels for a can't-miss gift.

At a Loss for Words. Tuck a gift certificate or money between the pages of a dictionary, with a note, "There aren't words enough to describe how much I love you."

A Gift in a Gift. Give a pair of gloves or socks, and hide your real gift inside either one. When giving an umbrella, slip a colorful knee sock onto each end and include some "bills" for a rainy day. Or, how about hiding a piece of jewelry in a jewelry box, back pocket in a pair of blue jeans, pencil case in a notebook, or in a change purse in a brand-new purse? It's always an added surprise to find a gift in a gift, and if you really want to go all out, hide more than one gift in a gift. In fact, the more the merrier!

Time to Unwind. Tie a gift certificate for a day at the spa to a ball of yarn that has been unwound all over the house. Attach the opposite end to a kitchen timer. Place the timer on the kitchen counter and be sure to hide the certificate somewhere else in the house. Add a note that says, "It's time to unwind! Follow me for some R&R."

A Hands-on Gift-Wrap Project. If your kids have made handprint plates or plaques for the grandparents, carry the theme out with the gift wrap. Cut paper grocery bags into sheets, place them inside out, and let the kids decorate them with their handprints.

Shine On. Place a piece of jewelry on a ribbon, and tie it around a flashlight. Tell her she lights up your life, brightens your world, or include a note that says, "I've really taken a shine to you."

O' Christmas Tree. If cash seems the most appropriate gift at Christmas, fanfold dollar bills and put a piece of ribbon or a pipe cleaner around the middle to create butterflies. Attach them to a tabletop Christmas tree. Deliver it with a card attached, "Who said money doesn't grow on trees?" Also, tie gift cards and money to ornaments for a creative presentation.

Minute-Made Gift Wrap. Hide a gift certificate, gift card, or money inside the sleeve of a videotape and tape it to the video. You can also do the same with a DVD or CD and *voila!* You have an instant gift wrap and two gifts in one.

Batter Up. Say "thank you" to a team mom with a batter bowl in which you've put a whisk plus a selection of lotions and aromatherapy candles. Tell her, "Batter up, it's the seventh-inning stretch, and time for you to relax."

"Egg-Stra" Special Delivery. Try using egg cartons as gift holders. Give a dozen votive candles, truffles, inexpensive jewelry, or an assortment of colorful socks or tiny collectibles for a child. Your card might read, "To an *egg-stra* special friend" or, "I hope this is *egg-zactly* what you wanted."

Screensaver. Here's a fun way to say you love her and is a gift in itself. Design a screensaver with photographs or a special quote. Install it when she is away from her computer. When she logs on, the screensaver will pop up and catch her by surprise.

Light of My Life. Give a silver candlestick with a gift certificate rolled up and put in the candle-holder, with a note, "Nobody else can hold a candle to you." This is also the ideal sentiment to add to a selection of beautiful candles.

"Sew" Much. Bury your gift in a box of thread, needles, and buttons, and add a note that says, "I love you *sew* much."

A Real Puzzle. Cut crossword puzzles out of the newspaper and duplicate them on a copy machine. Or, paste one on plain wrapping paper to wrap your gift. Write, "It's no puzzle why I think you're so special."

Pop the Question. If you're both sports fanatics, pop the question in front of the crowd. Most stadiums will let you propose in lights—on the huge scoreboard. You might even get your picture on national television. Better be

sure she'll say "yes" before trying this one! Or, check into renting a billboard to propose if money is no object. Or, do what one of my friends did for his wife and have a white park bench painted with your proposal and declaration of love. Have it placed where she'll unexpectedly find it. His said, "Lori, will you marry me? I love you, Arthur."

Out of the Box. It takes a special kind of person to appreciate this. Get up to six boxes of varying sizes that will fit one inside the other. Wrap the smallest with the gift enclosed, put it inside the next box, wrap it, and continue until you have them all inside the biggest box. Add a note to each box that says, "The best is yet to come"

Bed Brightener. Fill a bed tray that has pockets with magazines, a few crossword puzzles, specialty teas, shortbread cookies, breakfast jams, and anything that will brighten up the day for someone who is confined to bed rest.

Cyber Gift-Wrap. If he or she has a Web site, print out pages from the site and wrap up your gift with the online content. This also is a super suggestion for kids. All you have to do is print out a few pages from a favorite athlete, cartoon character, or celebrity's Web site for a clever web wrap-up.

Surprise, Surprise. Have the waiter deliver your gift during dinner for a special delivery. Or, hide a gift in his glove compartment, and leave him a note in his car to check it out. Gifts can be hidden almost anywhere ranging from her pocketbook or his briefcase. Or, tuck a letter with a special greeting in your kid's lunchbox or luggage when he or she is going to camp or college.

Noah's Ark. Fill a laundry basket or colorful toy box with an assortment of stuffed animals and a children's book about Noah's Ark. This colorful gift is perfect for a young party animal on your list. Add a pad of paper and markers so that he or she can make a buddy for each of the animals on board.

Hamper Pamper. Fill a baby hamper with gifts for the baby including towels, baby products, toys, and assorted items that are really useful. Add a great big bow for *a*

special delivery for *the* special delivery.

Your Ship Has Come In. Fill a large plastic toy ship with candy or small toys for a child, or attach a pair of engraved cufflinks or a watch to congratulate someone who has retired or whose "ship has come in." It's also a perfect way to give a gift to a nautical lover and include nautical coasters, candles, or ship-related items.

Suitcase Surprise. Fill a small, colorful suitcase with lots of little surprises that are gift-wrapped, and send it to a child who should select one surprise a day. The gifts will be enjoyed, and the suitcase will be useful for an on-the-go kid.

Top It Off. Slip a satin-and-lace garter around your engagement or wedding gift for an instant gift-wrap bow and creative touch. Hang an ornament on your holiday gift, and use a permanent marker to personalize it with the date. For young girls and teens, attach a hairbrush, comb, hair ribbons, clips, and bows to top off a gift with a special twist. Or, for guys attach a tool, hammer, or wrench to the top of his gift, and instead of clear tape use masking or duct tape for a guaranteed memorable gift wrap.

The Big One. Giving a major gift like a car, boat, motorcycle, or bicycle? This will take some planning, but when giving a car, don't stop short of a spectacular delivery. For example, substitute their old car with the new one later in the evening or middle of the night. When it's time to go to work and she goes to get in her car, she'll be caught by surprise! Or, add a sign to the item at a parking lot or dock that reads, "Take me home, Justin. I'm yours!" Or, after a special birthday or anniversary dinner, have the waiter deliver a key on a silver platter.

Y

Is for Young at Heart—Gifts for Seniors

You may think older folks have gotten it all, seen it all, and done it all, but they still love the treasured feeling of being cherished and remembered. When you're looking for gifts for senior citizens, remember possible physical limitations and needs, as well as the probability that they have most of the "things" they want and may be downsizing rather than accumulating possessions. Think of gifts with a purpose or gifts of time and service.

Remember, seniors have also been there and done most of that. They have less room for things and prefer for those they love and care about not to waste their money. So gifts have a greater challenge and should be practical and purposeful. Here are some ideas for seniors and anyone who is hard to please or who has it all.

I Can See Clearly Now. Make reading easier for a senior with fading eyesight. Give a lighted magnifying glass, the kind that hangs from a strap around the neck. It will make all sorts of chores easier, like paying bills, mending, and continuing loved hobbies like needlework.

Shout It Out. If your favorite senior no longer hears as well as he once did, give him an amplified phone. Add a note that says, "We're amplifying our love for you."

Freezer Pleasers. If your senior isn't able to cook like in the old days but loves a home-cooked meal, fill the freezer with her favorite recipes and do it her way. Low salt, no cholesterol, and please her to a tee. Let her also select which recipes she wants and plan a few weeks of meals when there's no time or energy to cook. Be sure to add detailed directions for thawing and heating in large black letters on each package.

Typecast. If he loves his computer, give him a keyboard with large letters to help him see what he's doing more easily.

Free Ride. If he no longer drives and has trouble getting around, commit a certain day and time to give him a few hours of your undivided attention for running errands.

Raising "Cane." If she hasn't grown accustomed to the need for help with balance, find her a decorated cane, perhaps carved or painted with flowers. You can also wrap one with ribbons and transform it. Tell her, "Don't go using this to raise cain!" If your senior uses a cane, give her one with a "headlight," so she can see where she's going at night.

Read All About It. Inquire about large-print editions of their favorite newspaper or magazine. Purchase a subscription for them and send a note, "We love you in an extra big way."

The Night Is Young. Give them a night on the town, complete with a limo to chauffeur them, a corsage, dinner and dancing, and a nightcap waiting when they get home.

What a Perk! If she is a coffee lover who grinds and perks her own coffee, find a unit that does both and saves on space. Or, choose another handy gadget or appliance that offers multiple features like a television set with a VCR and DVD combined into one.

Games People Play. Offer a selection of games they enjoyed years ago and have a family game night. From large-dot dominoes, a cribbage board with oversized pegs, checkers and chess, to jumbo-face playing cards and good old bingo. Add a motorized card shuffler for arthritic hands, and give your presence and time for an evening of nostalgic fun.

Music to Their Ears. If reading is no longer a possibility, give a CD or DVD player and a selection of books and music on tape. Include coupons for rentals at a convenient nearby location to accompany your gift.

Surf the Net. Is your senior afraid to try the computer? Enlist the aid of a young family member to offer instruction, with the promise of weekly visits for ongoing lessons.

Get a Grip. Many companies now make kitchen utensils and gardening tools with soft easy-grip handles. Give an assortment with the thought, "Hope these help you get a grip on things."

Snug as a Bug. Look for a soft, lightweight fleece or chenille throw to keep on the sofa for when he feels a bit chilly. Add a monogram for a personalized touch.

Jewel of a Gift. If traditional watchbands are just too difficult to maneuver, offer a band with easy-to-use closures. The same goes for treasured rings that no longer fit. Check with your local jeweler for special ways they can assist in making these items wearable and be sure to add safety catches for extra security.

Special Delivery. Offer a gift of service to an older neighbor. Leave a note saying you'll pick up their mail and papers when you're out walking each day, if they'd like the help. Remember, it's the little things that count.

Assisted Loving. Don't forget to pamper the elderly relative in an assisted-living facility. Limited space means gifts may be hard to choose, but you can give a small gift enhanced by your attention.

Bring a selection of notecards, stationery, pens, and stamps, and offer to help with correspondence.

Reach for the Ceiling. For anyone with high ceilings or high storage shelves, getting up on a chair can be a risky business. Purchase a gadget that makes reaching easier for grabbing out-of-reach items and changing ceiling light bulbs. On your card, write, "The sky's the limit with this contraption."

Save the Date. Ask a senior out for an afternoon or evening, complete with dinner and a movie. Tell them, "Nobody my age can touch your wit, wisdom, and all-around fun." If possible, make it a regular visit to give him something to look forward to. Begin a journal and record the wisdom he gives you each outing, and share it with him to demonstrate how valuable his advice is to you.

The Big Squeeze. Give a tube squeezer, a little gadget we could all use. It makes getting the toothpaste or ointment out of a tube a simple proposition. Add a note that says, "There's no one I'd rather squeeze than you!"

Sentimental Journey. Commission a portrait of the entire family and present it to the oldest generation with a booklet of memories and good wishes from all the younger members.

The Picture of Good Health. Make an easy-to-read chart detailing medications, exercise regimen, and doctor's visits. Surround it with a collage of family photos, and say, "We all want you to stay the picture of good health."

Just "Skidding." If your senior lives in a home with slippery surfaces like hardwood, tile, or linoleum, give a pair of nonskid slippers. Say, "I prefer you stay safe, no s-kidding."

Memory Bank. Ask your elderly relative to help you give a gift to future generations. Bring along a cassette recorder or a video recorder and encourage him or her to revisit the past with family history, anecdotes from his or her life, genealogy details, anything that will fascinate the family long after he or she is gone.

Mirror, Mirror on the Wall. Putting on makeup and shaving can be difficult with dimming eyesight. Give them a wall-mounted magnifying mirror, one with lights would be great. Add a note, "Mirror, mirror on the wall, who's

the fairest of them all? The answer is in this gift!"

Alarming! If they can't hear the alarm clock, but they have morning obligations, give them a nifty alarm clock with a superloud alarm, flashing lights, and a microphone pad that goes under the pillow to awaken them. Phones that vibrate are also available for the hard of hearing, so check out the options.

Why We Love Grandma. Ask the kids to write a letter to Grandma (and/or Grandpa) and express their love. Have the letters and a photograph of her and the kids framed together and give her an expression of affection that she will always treasure.

Eating Out. Find out where your senior likes to eat out. Give gift certificates to a variety of favorite restaurants in your senior's area. Include a menu from each place so he or she can review the choices ahead of time.

Beauty and the Bath. How about giving the luxury of sitting on a comfortable seat in the shower? Give him a folding bath seat he can feel secure about while showering. Add a note that says, "Here's the best seat in the house!"

If Life's a Game. Make a regular date to play board games, word games, or card games. This kind of exercise keeps the brain nimble and fresh. Say, "I may not win, but I know I can't lose spending time with you."

What a Trip. Consider a gift of an airline ticket, a getaway, or that family cruise they have always hoped to go on. Or, if your senior is a single, arrange for a trip with other seniors. There's always some part of the world a senior has only dreamed about going to, but make sure there are cancellation and money-back guarantees. Arrange all the details, reserve the date, and then throw in some travel insurance, just in case.

Complaint Department. Most of us have something to complain about, but seniors have time on their hands to notice it daily. Whether it's a home or apartment problem, association dues, the price of groceries, or even the cost of stamps, listen carefully and give a gift that reflects their biggest complaint and provides assistance to help fix it. The best gift of all is a caring ear and, whenever necessary or possible, nip the problem in the bud!

Z

Is for Zero-Cost Gifts

How many times have you heard, "It's the thought that counts"? While making a splash with a fancy, expensive gift is a thrill for the giver as well as the receiver, there are many times when the thought is the most important component of a gift. Make it appropriate, make it clever, make it original, and it will be remembered long after the perfume is used up, the crystal broken, and the money spent. Give of yourself. There are many options you can give with zero or minimal cost, with time and effort as your major expenditure. Use things you already have to create new and exciting gifts. You will be well-rewarded for your thoughtfulness.

Consider your talents and skills. Perhaps you are a great cook and have a friend who needs a few culinary tips. Or, you have a knack for rearranging furniture or getting organized. Offer your time and talents and just watch the appreciative reaction. Just because it didn't cost a pretty penny, doesn't mean it's not a terrific gift. In fact, many gifts require your presence and time, and are often the most appreciated gifts of all.

Sew What? If they wear glasses or have aging eyes but still love to sew, thread up some needles and present a variety of threaded needles in different colors on a pincushion. This gift will certainly be enjoyed in the stitch of time.

My First Library Card. Make this a big treat to be proud of. Give your child his or her own wallet to hold the library card, and reinforce how proud you are. Make weekly trips to the library and unlock a world of wonder.

Give an Acrostic. Words are free and fabulous and offer a unique opportunity to make someone feel special. Create what's called "an acrostic" and use the first letters of a person's name or a special word to spell out a phrase that reflects how you feel about him or her. Print it on a pretty piece of paper and frame it. Here are a few examples:

Jen:
Just a jewel of an
Encouraging editor and
Naturally nice!

Doug:
Devoted and dedicated,
One
Unbelievably unique uncle and
Great guy.

Ali:
Always amazing Ali
Loves to laugh and
Is incredible and interesting!

First-Class Teacher. If you know from the beginning that your child is just going to love his teacher, keep a journal for the teacher. Record the wonderful things your child says about her, including details of projects, class trips, and activities. Pass the book to other parents to do the same throughout the year. Make a scrapbook at the end of the year, and present it to the teacher with a card, "To a first-class teacher!"

Teacher Feature. If you feel your child's teacher has really made a difference, don't just tell her. Tell the world, or better yet *her* world. Write a letter to her principal and to the head of the school board, outlining why you think this teacher is an outstanding educator and a credit to her profession, and send her a copy.

Shop Till You Drop. Order an assortment of free catalogs on a variety of topics, or specific ones like gardening, and roll them up in a clay pot or a pretty vase. Give them to your supershopping friend.

What Are You Great At? Give the gift of your talents, regardless of what they might be. Whether you are brilliant at organizing drawers and closets, or have a knack for decorating or baking, offer your talents and time unconditionally. You'll never know how much your "two cents" and helpful efforts will be appreciated.

Compute This. Computer wizards, take note! Perhaps a grandparent or friend has a new computer and needs a few lessons at the very least. Offer your talents and time to teach him or her how to navigate cyberspace and beyond. Or, research someone's favorite topic of interest and print out related articles as well as locating resources online pertaining to things he or she collects.

Comic Relief. Clip cartoons, funny stories, and amusing articles from magazines and newspapers. Choose those you think will bring a smile to a friend's face. Paste them on paper and make a book filled with comic relief.

Notable Notes. Are you computer literate? Use your computer to create personalized stationery. You can find plenty of free graphics on the net. Add the recipient's name and address, and you've got a lovely and useful gift.

Mini Wishes. Do you travel? Save the miniature toiletries supplied by hotels for your use. You may put them in a box and give them to a friend, customized with new labels you create on the computer, exclusively for her with her name. Or, save them as a charitable gift to a women's shelter or home.

Make Her Day. One of the nicest gifts you can give is a specific compliment that truly reflects someone's efforts or hard work. Write a note telling someone how much you appreciate them, how great they look, or what a terrific job

they did on a recent project. Words of praise will enhance her days!

When Your Presence Is the Present. Just show up. Maybe he's lonely, or sick in bed, or injured. Did she lose her job? Be there, to listen, to be a friend. Hide a note she'll easily find after you leave that says, "Everybody needs somebody sometime. And I know you'll be there when it's my turn to need a friend."

Tag It. The holidays are fast approaching, and your budget is drained. What can you do? Make colorful gift tags to send as gifts. If you've got a computer, you can create and print them. If not, cut out the pictures from recycled greeting cards and hang them on gifts or glue them onto card stock. Add "To" and "From" in your best handwriting.

Virtually Fabulous. If both of you are computer savvy, send a virtual gift. You can choose from gorgeous floral bouquets, photos of faraway vacation spots, boxes of chocolates, bottles of champagne. Remember, these are just pictures, but they're a great way to say for free exactly what's on your mind or in your heart.

E-Mail Can Be E-xciting. Another way to save money is to send greeting cards via e-mail. Many sites will let you select an appropriate card for birthdays, anniversaries, Valentine's Day, or just about any celebration you can imagine. You add a personal sentiment, and zip, it's off to your recipient's computer in seconds.

A Gift with Wheels. You're going shopping anyway, so offer to take a less-mobile person with you. They'll appreciate the gesture, and you'll appreciate the company. Tell him, "Your presence is a gift to me."

Buy One, Get One Free. Next time you see an offer for an item you like, purchase one and save the other as a freebie for a friend. Or, if you spot a bargain or super-savings, call a friend and see if she wants you to pick up some for her, too.

In Remembrance of Things Past. Go through your photos and pull out ones someone will enjoy. Make a scrapbook, writing anecdotes of your memories, and present it, "In remembrance of days gone by."

Clipping Coupons. If you're an avid coupon clipper, make up a batch for a gift. Using envelopes, separate the coupons into categories, put them all into a larger envelope, and label it, "Good cents savings from me to you."

The Gift of Gab. Sometimes another person is hungry for someone to talk to. Call often and remember your presence is a gift. Your gift in return is the knowledge that you are cheering up another soul.

Word Share. If you've read a book and dearly loved it, share with a friend. Wrap it in pretty paper and give it with a note, "I devoured this book, and I know a bookworm like you will enjoy digesting it, too."

Roses of Love. Recycle flowers you receive and hang them upside down to dry. Arrange the fully dried flowers in a vase and give them as a gift.

Herb Garden. Harvest mint, basil, thyme, sage, and whatever else you grow in your herb garden. Let it air dry for a day or two, then put it in small bottles or even ziplock bags. Copy favorite recipes using the herbs, and give them as a gift with a note, "It's thyme to thank you for being such a good friend."

A List of Lists. A favorite gift of mine that is really helpful is to give a list of my favorite things. From my favorite beauty products, to where I love to find bargains, to where I surf online, these lists are considered a goldmine for the shopping impaired or a gift-giving diva. Instead of sending a holiday card, send your list for a welcome surprise.

Go Shopping in Your Closet. It's free and, believe it or not, treasures await you. Team up with a friend and spend a few hours in each of your closets. Try on outfits, and let your buddy rate them yes, no, or maybe. Donate the no's, and group the ones in question for a rainy day or for Halloween. This is a great way to get a second opinion on clothes you've outgrown and are reluctant to part with. If you have teenagers, encourage them to do the same and give their hand-me-downs to friends' kids or to a good cause.

Deals and Steals. There are slews of deals at local stores that offer frequent-shopper coupons. Collect duplicates of these coupons and share them with someone special for supersavings.

Talent Search. If you have a friend with a special talent like singing, dancing, modeling, or acting, search for local tryouts and inform her with a note saying you believe in her. An encouraging word will be the best gift at all, and you never know. You just might inspire and help launch the next huge superstar.

Special Dates I Wish to Remember

January

_____
_____
_____
_____
_____

February

_____
_____
_____
_____
_____

March

_____
_____
_____
_____
_____

April

_____
_____
_____
_____
_____
_____

May

_____
_____
_____
_____
_____
_____

June

_____
_____
_____
_____
_____
_____

July

_____

August

_____

September

_____

October

_____
_____
_____
_____
_____
_____

November

_____
_____
_____
_____
_____
_____

December

_____
_____
_____
_____
_____
_____

The Giftionary VIP Record

Name: _____
Telephone & email address: _____
Mailing address: _____
Birthday and other special days: _____
Sizes, likes & dislikes: _____
Hobbies & special interests: _____
Previous Gifts Given: _____
Previous Gifts Received: _____

Name: _____
Telephone & email address: _____
Mailing address: _____
Birthday and other special days: _____
Sizes, likes & dislikes: _____
Hobbies & special interests: _____
Previous Gifts Given: _____
Previous Gifts Received: _____

Name: _____
Telephone & email address: _____
Mailing address: _____
Birthday and other special days: _____
Sizes, likes & dislikes: _____
Hobbies & special interests: _____
Previous Gifts Given: _____
Previous Gifts Received: _____

Name: _____
Telephone & email address: _____
Mailing address: _____
Birthday and other special days: _____
Sizes, likes & dislikes: _____

Name: _____
Telephone & email address: _____
Mailing address: _____
Birthday and other special days: _____
Sizes, likes & dislikes: _____
Hobbies & special interests: _____
Previous Gifts Given: _____
Previous Gifts Received: _____

Name: _____
Telephone & email address: _____
Mailing address: _____
Birthday and other special days: _____
Sizes, likes & dislikes: _____
Hobbies & special interests: _____
Previous Gifts Given: _____
Previous Gifts Received: _____

Name: _____
Telephone & email address: _____
Mailing address: _____
Birthday and other special days: _____
Sizes, likes & dislikes: _____
Hobbies & special interests: _____
Previous Gifts Given: _____
Previous Gifts Received: _____

Name: _____
Telephone & email address: _____
Mailing address: _____
Birthday and other special days: _____
Sizes, likes & dislikes: _____
Hobbies & special interests: _____
Previous Gifts Given: _____
Previous Gifts Received: _____

Name: _____
Telephone & email address: _____
Mailing address: _____
Birthday and other special days: _____
Sizes, likes & dislikes: _____
Hobbies & special interests: _____
Previous Gifts Given: _____
Previous Gifts Received: _____

Name: _____
Telephone & email address: _____
Mailing address: _____
Birthday and other special days: _____
Sizes, likes & dislikes: _____
Hobbies & special interests: _____
Previous Gifts Given: _____
Previous Gifts Received: _____

Name: _____
Telephone & email address: _____
Mailing address: _____
Birthday and other special days: _____
Sizes, likes & dislikes: _____
Hobbies & special interests: _____
Previous Gifts Given: _____
Previous Gifts Received: _____

Name: _____
Telephone & email address: _____
Mailing address: _____
Birthday and other special days: _____
Sizes, likes & dislikes: _____
Hobbies & special interests: _____
Previous Gifts Given: _____
Previous Gifts Received: _____

Name: _____
Telephone & email address: _____
Mailing address: _____
Birthday and other special days: _____
Sizes, likes & dislikes: _____
Hobbies & special interests: _____
Previous Gifts Given: _____
Previous Gifts Received: _____

Name: _____
Telephone & email address: _____
Mailing address: _____
Birthday and other special days: _____
Sizes, likes & dislikes: _____
Hobbies & special interests: _____
Previous Gifts Given: _____
Previous Gifts Received: _____

Name: _____
Telephone & email address: _____
Mailing address: _____
Birthday and other special days: _____
Sizes, likes & dislikes: _____
Hobbies & special interests: _____
Previous Gifts Given: _____
Previous Gifts Received: _____

Name: _____
Telephone & email address: _____
Mailing address: _____
Birthday and other special days: _____
Sizes, likes & dislikes: _____
Hobbies & special interests: _____
Previous Gifts Given: _____
Previous Gifts Received: _____

VIP Sources

Favorite Stores

_____

_____

_____

_____

_____

_____

Favorite Online Shopping Sites

_____

_____

_____

_____

_____

_____

Favorite 1-800 Numbers

_____

_____

_____

_____

_____

_____

Notes

Index

puzzles, 44
stuffed animals, 44
superhero-themed comic books, 44–45
treasure basket, 46
two-way monitor, 45
worry beads, 46
writing papers and stationary, 43–44
gift delivery and wrapings, 153–58
baby hamper, 157
batter bowl, 155
bed tray, 156
boxes of varying sizes, 156
child's suitcase, 157
Christmas tree, 155
cookie bags, 154
crossword puzzles, 156
dictionary, 154
egg cartons, 155
gift delivered by waiter, 157
Gift Fairy, 153
gloves or socks, 154–55
large gifts, 158
Noah's Ark, 157
orange juice container, 154
plastic toy ship, 157
red roses, 153–54
ribbon trail, 153
satin-and-lace garter, 157–58
scoreboard proposals, 156
screensaver, 155–56
sewing kit, 156
silver candlestick, 156
stuffed teddy bear, 154
suitcases, briefcases, gym-bags, 154
tennis-ball can, 154
videotape, 155
web site pages, 156–57
yarn trail, 153
gift sources, 179
golden anniversary, 6
"come as you were" anniversary party, 6
Hawaiian fiftieth anniversary getaway, 6
letter "L" gifts, 6
stamps, 6
golfers, gifts for, 23
granddads
books, 29
grandchildren, giving phone card to, 28
Grandparents' Day, 115
hard-of-hearing telephone, 78–79
household chores, volunteering, 29
nostalgic gifts, 28–29
personalized refrigerator magnets, 28
scrapbook, 29
"thank you" note to, 128

See also dads; family and friends;
grandmothers
grandmothers, 78–79
gift certificates, 79
gold chain with hearts representing children
and grandchildren, 78
Grandparents' Day, 115
hard-of-hearing telephone, 78–79
magnifying make-up mirror, 78
memory book, 78
practical items, stocking up on, 78
telephone with large numbers on the dial,
78
"thank you" note to, 128
women, rules for buying gifts for, 75–76
See also family and friends; granddads; kids;
moms
Grandparents' Day, 115
grief, quotations relating to, 102
groomsman gifts, 149
engraved gifts, 149
flower photograph, 149
See also bridesmaid gifts; engagement gifts;
shower gifts; wedding gifts
Groundhog Day, 112

hhh
hairdressers, gifts for, 21
Hajj, 114
Halloween, 116–17
parties, 94
Hanukkah, 51–53, 117
bright and colorful themed gifts, 51–52
chocolate chip cookies, 2–53
college care package, 52
dreidels, 52
each night, special gifts representing, 53
family "together" gift, 53
homemade Hanukkah candies, 52
latke mix and applesauce, 52
synagogue gift shops, 53
happiness, 103
Hawthorne, Nathaniel, 103, 106
heartfelt gifts, 107–10
birthstone necklace, 108
blind, reading to,109
cause, walking for, 108–9
charitable contributions, 107
children's charities or hospital, giving gifts
to, 108
clothing drives, 108
correspondence, helping senior citizen's
with, 109
firemen and policemen, honoring, 108
forgiveness, 110

mood ring, 62
name necklace, 62
#1 pin or pendant, 60
pearl pendant necklace, 68
pearls, strand of, 61–62
religious symbol jewelry, 62
ring accompanied with a song, 61
sonic jewelry cleaner, 63
studs, 61
tiger's eye, 61
toe ring, 61
wristwatch, 62
See also birthstones
Johnson, Samuel, 102, 103, 104

kkk
Keller, Helen, 101
kids (toddlers to teens), 64–70
automobile trips, 66
baseball stadium, first trip to, 66
books for teens, 69
books for tots, 65
camping gear for Scouting trips, 66
car wash coupons, 68
care packages, 69
CD or DVD, 68
charm bracelet, 67
concert or theater tickets, 68
crib to bed, move to, 65
duffle bags, 69
first bike, 65–66
first day of school, 65
first haircut, 65
gift certificates, 68
half-birthdays, 66
name, gifts starting with each letter of, 66–67
new babies and older siblings, 65
number related gifts, 66
pearl pendant necklace, 68
personalized thank-you notes, 67
prepaid phone cards, 68–69
private telephone, 67–68
rÈsumÈ, helping organize, 68
safety gadgets, 69
security blankets, 65
shopping coupons, 69
spa treatments, 70
stuffed cow as "goodbye" gift, 67
stuffed lamb as "back soon" gift, 67
sweets, 67
Tooth Fairy pillow, 66
videocamera, 69
kindness, quotations relating to, 103–5
Kipling, Rudyard, 103

Kwanzaa, 53–54, 118
creativity and, 54

lll
Labor Day, 115
last-minute gifts, 71–74
bag of snacks, 72
bargain Christmas ornaments, 73
birthday facts and miscellany, 73
cash in a balloon, 72
flowers, 73
freezer, storing edible gifts in, 73
gift closet, 71
home-cooked dinner, gift certificate for, 73
houseplants, 73
ice cream toppings, 72
jar of mint, 72–73
magazine subscription, 71–72
magnifying mirror, 73
pears in a basket, 72
phone card, 72
pocket-sized tools, 73
recipes, 72
restaurant reservations, 73
shopping spree, 72
undivided attention, gift coupon for, 72
video rental gift cards, 73
virtual gift certificate, 73
lawyers, gifts for, 21
loneliness (gifts that express), 56–57
blue items, 57
dictionary, 57
photograph, 57
teddy bear, 57
Longfellow, Henry Wadsworth, 102
love, quotations relating to, 105

mmm
making a difference, quotations relating to, 106
manicurists, gifts for, 22
marriage, quotations relating to, 105
Martin Luther King Day, 111–12
May Day, 114
Memorial Day, 114
memory makers. See party favors
men. See dads; granddads
Moliere, 102
moms, 76–78
assorted nuts, 76
blank journal for recipes, 76
book of days, 76
china setting, addition to, 76
desk accessories, 76
e-mail lessons, 76
Mother's Day, 114

Other books by
Robyn Freedman Spizman
www.robynspizman.com

When Words Matter Most: Thoughtful Words and Deeds to Express Just the Right Thing at Just the Right Time

Women for Hire: The Ultimate Guide to Getting a Job (with Tory Johnson and Lindsey Pollak)

Life's Little Instruction Book for the Incurable Romantic (with H. Jackson Brown, Jr.)

Getting Through to Your Kids (with Dr. Michael Popkin)

A Hero in Every Heart (with H. Jackson Brown, Jr.)

300 Incredible Things for Women on the Internet (with Ken Leebow)

300 Incredible Things to Learn on the Internet (with Ken Leebow)

The Thank You Book

Getting Organized

Free and Fabulous

Quick Tips for Busy People

Monsters Under the Bed and Other Childhood Fears (with Drs. Stephen and Marianne Garber)

Good Behavior (with Drs. Stephen and Marianne Garber)

Beyond Ritalin (with Drs. Stephen and Marianne Garber)

If Your Child Is Hyperactive, Inattentive, Impulsive, Distractible . . . Helping the ADD/Hyperactive Child (with Drs. Stephen and Marianne Garber)